Sunrise After Rain

Regina Arnold

Published by Regina Arnold, 2024.

While every precaution has been taken in the preparation of this book, the publisher assumes no responsibility for errors or omissions, or for damages resulting from the use of the information contained herein.

SUNRISE AFTER RAIN

First edition. May 28, 2024.

Copyright © 2024 Regina Arnold.

Written by Regina Arnold.

Table of Contents

INTRODUCTION

To the mothers whose lives have been unwillingly transformed:

It's my belief that from the moment a baby is conceived, an enduring, sacred connection is forged between mother and child. The best way I can describe it is like a tapestry woven with highs and lows, laughter and worry, love and fear. Every milestone, every giggle, every scraped knee adds another thread, a vibrant mix of emotions forever tied together.

When the unthinkable happens, our motherhood is irrevocably changed. The once vibrant fabric of life becomes stained with tears. The vivid hues of happiness fade into a somber gray, leaving behind a reality that feels impossible to confront. That woman who once skipped joyfully through life, hand in hand with her child, now treads a path marked by sorrow. Each tear she sheds is a reflection of the emptiness left behind, a testament to the indelible mark of grief.

However, there will come a time when she rises like a phoenix from the ashes, born from the love and loss that have shaped her. Despite her burden, she walks with her head held high, an affirmation of the unwavering love between her and her child. Though her life is forever altered, she continues to move forward, to heal and evolve.

With the sudden passing of my adult son, Steve, in 2021, my world was fundamentally reshaped. Sadness threatened to consume me, so I had to find a tangible way to connect with him in his absence from my daily life. On the many nights when I couldn't sleep, I turned to writing him letters – expressions of love, anger, sadness, regret, joy, and more, from the depths of my soul to his.

These letters were subsequently shared with the world, revealing that my personal journey of healing resonated with those in search of hope amidst their own experience of loss. Sharing my story fostered a connection between my grief and the hearts of others navigating their own darkness.

I want to express my heartfelt appreciation to you for choosing to buy this book. When I began writing it, I didn't have a clear plan, but I knew it would be more than just my story; it's about the power of shared experiences. It combines parts of my own personal path from my journal and blog, as well as the valuable insights and strength that other mothers have shared. Collectively, all these elements came together to create a meaningful and expressive book.

As you read this, may you find strength, hope, healing, and tranquility in the understanding that love and loss can coexist.

P.S. - Each chapter is like a letter straight from my heart to yours. Think of them as little stepping stones on your personal healing journey. Feel free to explore, pick what feels right for your soul, and just let go of the rest.

TWO REASONS

"A wife who loses a husband is called a widow. A husband who loses a wife is called a widower. A child who loses his parents is called an orphan. There is no word for a parent who loses a child. That's how awful the loss is." ~ Jay Neugeboren

Dearest You,

Despite the loving intentions behind others' attempts to console us, the loss of a child leaves a wound that no mere words can mend. For those of us trying to map out the uncharted territory of this profound loss, while in its early stages, such remarks can be disappointing. For me, it was comments like "everything happens for a reason" and "be grateful that you had him as long as you did" that only served to amplify the emptiness.

Don't get me wrong. This doesn't mean people don't care, but it *can* cause some misunderstandings, especially when your grief is still raw. Which is why I believe in openly discussing this experience, not to blame anyone, to play the martyr or victim, but to create a more supportive environment for those who are going through this kind of heartache.

I say this for two reasons:

1. You have a mountain of work ahead of you. When the shock wears off and you step out from behind that curtain, your heart and mind switch to survival mode. You're left wondering, "What do I do now without my child by my side?" You're searching for an answer that only you can provide. While your spirituality or religion might bring you some solace, the question of "why" will always linger.

This question will resurface on the anniversary of their death, every birthday, and each time you're excited about something you wish you could share with them.

In my experience, it's essential to listen to my own inner voice during challenging times. Although empathy can be found in shared experiences, it's unrealistic to expect friends and loved ones who haven't gone through similar pain to fully understand. This realization led me to seek support from communities and resources dedicated to understanding and coping with this kind of loss.

2. There's no such thing as a complete recovery. This isn't a physical surgery you've been through. Or an accident, where you'll make a complete recovery. No, it's a blow to your very soul. Some days I felt like someone had blindfolded me, put a target on my chest and shot an arrow into the center of the bull's eye. I didn't see the arrow coming and had no way to defend myself.

Yes, the pain gets a little softer with time and implementing mindful self-care, but time doesn't always feel linear and healing is a forever journey. Borrowing from another Mom's description, it's like a spiral or a jagged graph of peaks and valleys. Sometimes it's like a race car doing 120 on the outside lane at the race track and other times it's like Grandma on the freeway moving slower than molasses on a cold winter day.

But if you, like me, hold onto the belief that you'll be reunited with your child someday, remember that it's not your time to depart yet. While you await that day, you still have a purpose to fulfill. For now, let your healing commence.

When you're in pain, close your eyes and smile, imagine your child sending you kisses and cheering you on, gently whispering in your ear, "You'll be okay, Mom."

PHONE HOME

"There are no goodbyes for us. Wherever you are, you will always be in my heart." ~ Ghandi

Dearest You,

When it first happens, we're in shock, disbelief, confusion, and we question our sanity. We ask ourselves, "Did this really happen? Why did he die?"

If it was easy to find your "center" again after the passing of your child, there would be no need for grief support. No need for a connection with other grieving mothers and fathers. But as you and I both know, there's nothing easy about any of this. It's a desolating, overwhelming experience; one that we never dreamed would happen to us.

And like in the E.T. movie, we just want to phone home. We're looking for that place that was once filled with our child. We want to be there again and stay there. We cringe at the idea of being part of a "grieving parents" club.

We question why we're still here and our child isn't. Yet, somewhere in the deepest part of our being, there's a knowing that we're alive right now in this time and space for a reason; a purpose. We just haven't been able to phone home yet to find out exactly what that is.

How do you get your answers? It's different for everyone. Some pray, some meditate, some consult a therapist or hypnotherapist, a psychic or medium, and some do nothing, attempting to take this on alone. But the one thing most parents do, at some point when they feel the time is right to find their center is join a grief support group. When you choose the right group for you, you'll often find yourself surrounded by a shared love like you've never experienced before.

Maybe not the first one or two times you attend, but it will happen if you're open to it. The first time I went to a grief support gathering, I realized I'd just entered a room filled with broken hearts. But as I kept going, I discovered this was my community, my new tribe.

Perhaps your center lies within a community like this, too, where healing becomes your focus, and at some point, you share your healing with others. Who knows? This might just be the reason you're here.

LAYERS OF GRIEF

"Grief is a process, not a destination. It changes and evolves over time, becoming a part of your story rather than your entire story." ~ Megan Devine

Dearest You,

In 1969, Elizabeth Kubler-Ross introduced the five stages of grief in her book *On Death and Dying,* which include denial, anger, bargaining, depression, and acceptance. In my personal experience, these stages often feel more like layers, with one stage sometimes piling on top of another and, at times, all blending together.

The initial layer for me was shock and disbelief, particularly because my son died so suddenly. But even when a loss is anticipated, such as a terminal illness, it feels impossible to accept the reality at first. You may feel numb or like you're trapped in a nightmare. This is a natural human response to death, and it's crucial to allow yourself sufficient time to process the "event."

The second layer entails sadness and anger. You may experience heartbreak, rage, or a combination of both. I can attest to feeling both intensely. I screamed, cried, and lashed out, most often when I was alone in my car. The pain was so profound and exposed that it left me breathless. I now understand that these emotions are typical for a mother struggling with the unimaginable. However, as I discovered, lashing out isn't an ideal solution, especially while driving – like the time I was going to an appointment when a wave of grief ambushed me and I ran a red light. Quite an expensive lesson to learn!

The third layer of grief is guilt and regret. At first, you may feel guilty simply because you're still here and your child isn't. You may also feel guilty for things you did or didn't do and things you said or didn't say. And you may regret that there are things you'll never get to do with your child. These feelings are also natural, a way of trying to make sense of what happened.

The fourth layer is loneliness and isolation. You may feel like you're the only one going through this pain, like you've lost your place in the world; that you don't belong, like your whole being is crumbling. These feelings are normal as well, but these are the ones that can make you feel isolated, because withdrawing feels like the right thing to do to protect yourself. (I'll address isolation in depth in a later chapter).

The fifth layer of grief is hope and healing. As you move forward along your journey, you begin to find glimmers of hope. You may start to think about your future, and develop healthy ways to cope. Keep in mind, this is not a linear process and naturally there will be detours, twists and turns along the way. But eventually you'll begin to explore what a new normal looks like for you.

One Mom that I met on this journey is an artist and described her grief like a kaleidoscope, constantly shifting and changing, with each turn revealing a new pattern. Just as a kaleidoscope's colors, shapes, and reflections blend together to create a beautiful and intricate design, so too do our emotions blend together to form the complex tapestry of grief. The shards of glass within a kaleidoscope represent the fragments of our heart, reflecting and refracting light as we navigate the emotional labyrinth of loss.

That got me thinking about the triggers and ambushes I've experienced as part of the grieving process, unexpectedly revisiting the various layers of grief due to certain situations. This can occur when you encounter a smell, a picture, a specific time of day, or an item in a store that reminds you of your child. Please be compassionate with yourself during these moments, allowing the emotions to surface and acknowledging that it's a natural part of the healing journey.

Let this be your reminder that there's no right or wrong way to grieve and there's no set timeline for recovery. Listen to your heart and give it ample time to heal.

YOUR NEEDS ARE?

―――

"Taking care of yourself doesn't diminish your grief, it allows you to process it." ~ Unknown

Dearest You,

It's an understatement to say that grief is a draining experience, impacting us emotionally, physically and mentally. That's the reason it's crucial to explore methods to replenish our inner resources in order to effectively cope with our loss. The various layers of grief can have a detrimental effect on our well-being without us even realizing it, particularly in terms of our health. So, how can you strengthen your inner core?

One way to prioritize your well-being is to put your physical health at the top of your to-do list. This includes getting sufficient sleep (I know how hard that is sometimes), adopting a healthy diet, and engaging in regular exercise – even if it's just a leisurely walk around the neighborhood or doing chair yoga.

When you prioritize your physical well-being, you're better equipped to manage stress and exhaustion, two significant factors that can negatively impact your journey through grief. Compare it to the fuel in your car. If you neglect to refuel, you'll soon be running on fumes, and then the car's indicator will suddenly flash "E" and ultimately shut down. Always monitor your energy levels.

Don't put off the things that make you happy. This could include listening to music, reading, cuddling with a pet, or spending time in nature. Doing things that you enjoy can help boost your mood and energy levels. I know it sounds rather trite, but your child really *would* want you to enjoy your life again.

A lot of times we have a tendency to stuff our feelings, holding it all in, so that we can put the people in our inner circle first, and that's OK. But there's only so many hours in a day. So make sure to include self-care as part of your daily routine.

Why not immerse your tired body in a long, hot shower with a sea salt scrub, take a scented bubble bath, get a massage, read a book, or just close the bedroom door to temporarily shut out the world and take a nap? How will your body and soul heal if you don't give yourself time to rest? Relaxation periods for yourself are a must, not *maybe when I have time.*

Show yourself some patience. Grief is not a race to the finish line. Accept that it takes as long as it takes. There's no time clock or someone standing on the sidelines with a stop-watch. Allow yourself to feel your emotions and don't be afraid to ask for help when you need it. I learned the hard way that taking care of myself first is a strength, not a weakness.

Here are some additional things you can do to meet your needs:

Stay hopeful. It may be difficult to see the light at the end of the tunnel right now, but it's important to stay hopeful for the future. Trust that you *will* eventually heal from your loss.

Focus on the positive memories of your child. Thinking about the good times you shared can help you cope with your grief. It's OK to smile and laugh as you remember those cherished moments you had together.

Celebrate their life. This could mean holding a memorial service or celebration of life, planting a tree in their honor, and writing them letters. In my case, writing letters to Steve was my method of giving voice to my silent screams and, believe me, there were many.

Find meaning in your loss. Helping others who are grieving, volunteering for a worthy cause, or starting a foundation can also provide you with ways to turn your pain into purpose.

Self-appreciation. Take a few minutes once a day that you can dedicate to yourself. Find a comfortable, quiet place and bring a pen and paper or journal. Write a note of appreciation to yourself, recognizing how far you've come to where you are right now.

Even in this digital world, I recommend handwriting because the slower pace and focus required can create a more mindful state, allowing you to be more present with your thoughts and emotions as you write. This increased self-awareness can further deepen the connection between your inner world and your outer one. It requires more focus and concentration than typing, but this focused state allows you to delve deeper into your emotions and express them more authentically.

Studies have shown that writing by hand involves certain brain regions that are not typically activated when typing. The physical act of forming letters on paper can enhance emotional expression, providing a richer sensory experience than typing on a keyboard. You can even add to your experience by drawing pictures, using colored pencils, and markers. One Mom told me she uses crayons to draw pictures in her journal because her daughter loved them and she visualizes her daughter smiling as she creates them. But whatever method you choose, pour appreciation into who you are and all that you do.

Grief is a heavy, difficult journey, but it's one that you *can* get through. By taking care of yourself and finding healthy ways to nurture your mind, body, and soul, you can get your needs met and reclaim your inner strength.

SYNCHRONICITY?

Dearest You,

At some point, you may start noticing signs and synchronicities like I have. When my son's military memorial service was coming closer, I found myself feeling anxious and fidgety. I know it was because it felt like this would be my final goodbye.

I remember my voice weak and shaking during the conversation I had with the Army Captain who told me what would happen at Steve's service. A chaplain would give the invocation, followed by the ceremonious folding of the U.S. flag, a rifle volley, and the playing of TAPS. Even at the mention of TAPS, the lump in my throat felt like a golf ball. If you've ever heard that mournful melody, you know what I mean.

A couple of days before his service, I set out to find two small American flags to place at his grave. Even though I know on each holiday, the National Cemetery will place flags at each service member's gravesite, I still wanted to place them myself on his. It's a special day and my way of thanking him for his courageous service to our country.

I went to several stores, looking for just the right size, but found nothing that was suitable. The search had become disappointing and I was tired, so I thought I'd better get to the grocery store (my last stop before going home) and pick up some food items.

After checking out and heading toward the exit, I happened to look up at the Customer Service counter and there they were ... a container full of brand new flags, just the right size that I had been looking for. Mind you, I shop at that store all the time and have never seen them before. I smiled and cried at the same time.

There are no coincidences. There's no doubt in my mind that a divine force guided me to the right place at the right time.

THE POWER OF SMILING

<hr>

"Be the reason someone smiles. Be the reason someone feels loved and believes in the goodness in people." ~ Roy T. Bennett

Dearest You,

When you're in pain, I know it's awfully hard to smile, but did you know that smiling can stimulate your brain to release endorphins, which are natural mood enhancers? These happy hormones can help alleviate stress and anxiety, providing a sense of comfort and well-being.

Researchers at the University of Kansas published findings that smiling helps to reduce the body's response to stress and lowers the heart rate in anxious situations. Another study linked smiling to lower blood pressure, while another suggests that smiling leads to longevity. So, when you're feeling blue, try putting on a smile.

Here's a synopsis of their published findings:

- Smiling helps you live longer.

- Smiling relieves stress.

- Smiling elevates your mood.

- Smiling is contagious.

- Smiling boosts the immune system.

- Smiling may lower blood pressure.

- Smiling reduces pain.

- Smiling makes you attractive.

- Smiling suggests confidence.

- Smiling helps you stay positive.

Next time you're out, remember to smile at someone. This simple act of kindness can brighten up someone's day, and you're likely to receive a smile in return and that alone could make *your* day.

Even on those days when you're at home and want to be in hermit mode (I've been there a lot), try looking in the mirror and smiling at yourself, even if tears are filling your eyes. Tell yourself that you're worth feeling happy, because you most certainly are.

GRIEVING IN ISOLATION

"Remember, even the stars seem isolated, yet they shine together in the vastness of the night sky." ~ Unknown

Dearest You,

While it's normal to feel isolated and withdrawn from others while grieving, it's important to remember that social support is essential for your health.

That's the reason many people have found comfort in sharing their grief with others, however, some may still choose seclusion, especially in the early stages of their loss. There could be various reasons for this, like when you're feeling overwhelmed, exhausted, or burdened with trying to put on a brave face. Often this happens during and shortly after the funeral, when family, friends and well-wishers have gone back to their everyday lives.

Isolation during times of grief can have its benefits, but it's essential to consider the drawbacks as well —there are two sides to every coin. By choosing to be alone, you may experience heightened anxiety and depression, and coping with grief becomes more challenging when you lack support. The burden can feel utterly overwhelming.

Another significant drawback is the slower recovery that comes with isolation. That's why having access to people who offer understanding, empathy, and companionship can help us in recovering more quickly. They can guide us towards positive coping skills and encourage us to engage in activities that promote healing.

And when we combine grief with isolation, it's like a double whammy to our physical health. The absence of social connections can lead to unhealthy behaviors, including excessive smoking, drug use, alcohol overindulgence, and 'comfort' overeating. One Mom shared with me that she developed an addiction to alcohol, but after a while realized the damage it was causing. She said it numbed her pain at first, but only briefly until the next day, when she felt even worse.

These habits can contribute to chronic health problems like heart disease and stroke, further complicating an already devastating time. There was a period of time, in the second year after Steve's passing, that all I wanted to do was eat my go-to comfort food every night – mint chocolate chip ice cream and popcorn. Not a good idea. My tummy wasn't happy with me. Ouch!

However, there's a viable solution to address this issue. By fostering social connections and promoting a sense of community, we can minimize the negative consequences of social isolation. Having learned the hard way, I encourage you to engage in regular social interactions, whether in-person or through virtual platforms, as they offer many benefits. It not only helps combat unhealthy habits but also improves overall well-being and reduces the risk of chronic health problems. Implementing this solution provides an opportunity to live a healthier, more fulfilling, and empowered life in the face of loss.

Here are a few suggestions of things you can do to avoid isolation during grief:

- **Talk to someone you trust:** It's perfectly normal to feel overwhelmed when you're struggling with these unfamiliar emotions. Sharing your feelings with a trusted friend, family member, therapist, or grief counselor can provide a safe space to process your pain and connect with someone who understands. Their support can be invaluable as you begin to heal and move forward at your own pace.

● **Consider joining a grief support group:** Grief support groups can provide a safe and supportive environment to connect with other people who "get you" because they're grieving, too. I've learned so much from the group I've been attending.

● **Stay connected with social activities:** Try to maintain your usual social activities, even if you don't feel like it; even if it means taking baby steps to getting back out there. Spending time with loved ones can help you feel less alone and more supported, too. And don't hesitate to say "I could use a hug" when you're feeling fragile and need some tenderness.

● **Volunteer your time:** If possible for you, volunteering can be a great way to give back to your community and meet new people. It can also help you feel good about yourself and make a difference in the world.

It's understandable if you're feeling overwhelmed by your emotions right now. Just remember, you're not alone in your grief. There are people who care about you and want to help.

This reminds me of a beautiful excerpt from Martha W. Hickman's book, *Healing After Loss - Daily Meditations for Working Through Grief:*

There is a story of a little girl who got home from visiting her friend later than her mother had expected. When her mother asked the reason for the delay, the child said, *"I was helping Jane. Her doll broke."* The mother asked, "*Did you help her fix it?*" The child said, "*No, I helped her cry.*" We all need someone to help us cry.

Grieving isn't pretty, but having a friend who can be fully present when you need to cry, helps you ease your feelings of abandonment. If you're feeling isolated, please reach out for support.

I'M NOT A VICTIM; I'M GRIEVING

"Every breath I take is a reminder of your absence. My heart aches for you, my dear son, and the life we no longer get to share" ~ Unknown

Dearest You,

Grief makes almost everyone question their faith at one time or another, especially in the beginning. And even more so if your child's death happened suddenly.

When I found Steve in my home and knew that he was gone, I felt like God had snatched him right out of my life. He was here one minute and gone the next. No chance to say goodbye. I went into a rage, screaming, "God, please don't take him away! How could you *do* this to me?"

I initially perceived my loss as the consequence of a vengeful, punishing God. This perspective made me feel like a victim, consumed by guilt. And I was angry. Very angry. However, as time progressed, my thoughts on the matter evolved. Eventually, I experienced a sense of relief. I understood that living as a victim was not how I desired to spend the remainder of my life, nor would my son want me to be burdened by his passing.

What changed for me was the discovery of a grief support group composed of individuals sharing similar experiences. Through this, I came to realize:

- I wasn't going crazy; these emotions are normal.

- There are no "rules." Period.

- The grief timeline is long.

- No man or woman is an island.

- God isn't punishing me.

- I'm not a victim; I'm grieving.

Granted, nobody wants to be in that room full of broken hearts but, together with others going through the same thing, I found some much needed comfort and the strength to carry on.

Each time I left the group and walked to my car, I felt blessed for what I learned from those souls who were willing to share their stories, creating new threads in my tapestry. It wasn't long before I summoned the willingness to share my story, rather than holding it all in. It felt so good to be supported.

Since those early days, I've come to feel enormous gratitude for this group and many of them have told me that the things I've shared have had a positive impact on them, too. I think it's fair to say that destiny often places us in the appropriate place at the most opportune moment.

THERE'S NO TIMER

"The only people who think there's a time limit for grief have never lost a piece of their heart. Take all the time you need" ~ Unknown

Dearest You,

It's acceptable to grieve at the hospital. It's acceptable to grieve at the funeral home. It's acceptable to grieve at the grave site. But what happens after that?

Later, when the hospital, funeral home, and grave site are distant, murky memories, you're still grieving; still experiencing the tidal wave of emotions; still being triggered. Down the road, even though they may not say it, others may think it's time for you to pick up your life and move forward. Especially when they see you having some good days. You know ... the ones when you have a smile on your face and look like a calm ocean on a sunny day. What they don't see is that there are giant waves slamming the shore on the other side of that ocean. So you put on a brave face; a mask. But for whose benefit?

Behind the mask, you're still missing the physical presence of your beloved child; their essence, all the shared experiences with them. The things you'll never get to do with them in the future. And so much more. You get tired, worn out.

There are still sleepless nights, brain fog, and those many days without makeup because you know it will only get washed away with your tears. Dealing with people who think your grief should be "over" by now can be incredibly frustrating. And it's natural for us, too, to wonder how long this is going to last. So, what can you do?

Here are some tips on how to handle it:

Be honest. Gently explain that you're still grieving and haven't reached a point of closure. You can say something like, "I appreciate your concern, but I'm still trying to cope with my child's loss and it's not a linear process."

Limit your exposure. If individuals tend to make thoughtless remarks, it may be beneficial to limit your interaction with them. You are not obligated to justify your emotions to anyone.

Focus on your support system: Surround yourself with people who understand and validate your feelings. Talk to a therapist or grief counselor if needed.

Express your feelings: Let people know what kind of support you need, whether it's a listening ear, practical help, or just some personal space.

Ask for what you want: If someone offers to help, be specific about what would be helpful, like bringing a meal, mowing the lawn, running errands, or simply sitting with you.

Prioritize your well-being: Take care of your physical and emotional needs first. Eat healthy, get enough sleep, exercise, and engage in activities you enjoy. (I know when it comes to this, I sound like a broken record, but it's *so* important).

Be kind to yourself: Don't judge your feelings or pressure yourself to move on quicker than you're ready. Healing takes time and patience.

There's no timer for grief. Everyone deals with pain in their own way and everyone is entitled to do that without judgment from anyone else. Be kind to yourself and acknowledge your painful emotions. Don't put pressure on yourself to pretend you're "over it" when you're not.

STRUCTURE MAY BE NEEDED

"Grief changes us, but it does not define us. May you find the strength to emerge from this darkness and embrace life once more" ~ Unknown

Dearest You,

When grieving the loss of your child, you may forget to take focused care of your "self," to make *you* a priority. After all, it's understandable that there are other people's needs to attend to, especially if you have a spouse and other children in your home. One of the ways I'm doing it is to change things up and create a new and different physical exercise routine. The reason is twofold:

1. Structure is essential these days as grief can be a fluctuating experience, similar to a roller coaster. Emotions can rise and fall, with certain days proving to be more challenging than others. For me, Sundays are the most difficult, as it's the day my son passed away.

2. Exercise feeds the body and mind, creating endorphins, which helps to alleviate pain, even if it's only doing some stretching.

This may sound crazy (promise not to laugh?), but one of the tricks I've learned from another grieving Mom is to stand upright, shoulders straight, and begin jumping up and down. Shake your hands out, as if you're releasing those negative feelings out through your fingertips. Imagine those feelings are drops of water and feel free to shake them out all over the room. (Traumatic memories can stay locked inside your body for days, months, years, or forever). Physical exercise helps to move the stuck energy through your body.

One additional activity I've taken up, which I hadn't done since my junior high days, is the twist—yes, that timeless dance craze popularized by Chubby Checker. You can find the video on YouTube, guaranteed to make you smile, even if you're not comfortable actually doing the dance.

I hate it when people say "trust me" but, trust me, changing things up actually works. So do your best to lose your stress.

MY MOM LIES

"It's perfectly OK to admit you're not OK" ~ Unknown

Dearest You,

I found this poem on griefhaven.org, a site which has a lot of valuable resources that you may want to check out. I've listed a link for it, as well as others on the RESOURCES page at the end of this book.

This piece is specifically for us Moms and how we sometimes skirt the truth when asked how we're doing:

My Mom, she tells a lot of lies she never did before.

But from now until she dies, she'll tell a whole lot more.

Ask my Mom how she is and because she can't explain,

She will tell a little lie because she can't describe the pain.

Ask my Mom how she is. She'll say, "I'm alright."

If that's the truth, then tell me, why does she cry each night?

Ask my Mom how she is. She seems to cope so well.

She didn't have a choice, you see, nor the strength to yell.

Ask my Mom how she is. "I'm fine. I'm well. I'm coping."

For God's sake, Mom, just tell the truth. Just say your heart is broken.

She'll love me all her life. I loved her all of mine.

But if you ask her how she is, she'll lie and say she's fine.

I am here in Heaven. I cannot hug from here.

If she lies to you, don't listen. Hug her and hold her near.

On the day we meet again, we'll smile and I'll be bold.

I'll say, "You're lucky to get in here, Mom, with all the lies you told!"

If this poem hits home for you, know that sharing your genuine emotions of grief can be a liberating experience, providing an opportunity to form deeper connections with others. It's essential to recognize and appreciate the effort you're putting in to navigate this difficult time. Embracing your feelings and telling the truth will help you find comfort in the support of those who really understand and care for you.

THE HEALING POWER OF HUMOR

"I believe in the healing power of laughter. It forces us to breathe" ~

Brene Brown

Dearest You,

My son was a Microsoft Certified Systems Engineer. As you might know, engineers can be very analytical. Sometimes they can analyze things to the point of analysis paralysis. Haha! That was Steve.

A few months after his death, my daughter found a picture of him, standing in the backyard of their dad's farm, hands on his hips, staring down at a broken chain saw. We laughed out loud because we both knew, by the look on his face and how his analytical brain worked, that he was analyzing how he could repair it and he'd be thinking about it for at least 30 minutes. We called it his *30-minute face* and teased him about it on more than one occasion.

It was at that moment I realized I was allowing myself to laugh for the first time since his death. And I knew it was possible to heal.

Laughter, as they say, is the best medicine. Its therapeutic effects are well documented, and this extends to the realm of grief, too. Humor doesn't erase the pain of loss; but it can serve as a coping mechanism that helps us navigate our challenging emotions more gracefully.

Allowing a sense of humor into your life during times of grief might seem counterintuitive, but as I learned, it can be a powerful tool for healing and resilience. It reminded me that Steve's essence lives on in the stories I share about him. And when family and friends come together to share funny stories or light-hearted memories about the person they've lost, it creates an atmosphere of unity. Humor can serve as a bridge, offering an opportunity for communal healing.

So, just as you may have to give yourself permission to cry at times, please give yourself permission to laugh again.

LETTING GO OF GUILT

"Guilt is a burden that we can choose to release, for it serves no purpose in our journey towards growth and healing" ~ Unknown

Dearest You,

At some time during your grief journey, guilt can creep in and make you question if you could have done more, or if there was something you should have said but didn't, so it's essential to remember that nobody is perfect. We're all human and guilt is a normal feeling.

When my son suffered his heart attack, I attempted CPR, but sadly, I couldn't save him. I couldn't help but feel guilty for not recognizing how unusually quiet he was earlier that day. Perhaps he was feeling unwell and didn't want to worry me. Despite the reassurance from paramedics that there was nothing more I could have done, guilt hung over me like a dark cloud. I watched them shock his body six times with the paddles and use the EpiPen six times until they finally got a weak pulse and whisked him away in the ambulance. The time that elapsed between his cardiac arrest and bringing him back was 25 minutes.

I knew that his brain had been deprived of oxygen for far too long and, ultimately, brain scans showed extensive, irreparable damage. The neurologist said Steve would never be able to function on his own again, so this marked the beginning of the battle between my mind and my heart because I knew he wouldn't want to be kept alive by machines. It was then that I had to make the hardest decision a mother can ever make. Do I keep his body alive in a hospital bed, hooked up to life support or do I let him go? My heart knew his soul had already made the transition, so my daughter and I made the decision to let his body go, too. I can't even begin to express what that felt like.

The human mind uses logic and seeks order in the face of chaos, craves understanding and a sense of control. It searches for answers, struggles with all those 'what-ifs," and tries to make sense of the senseless.

The heart, however, is a different story. It's the seat of our emotions; that place that feels the full brunt of our loss. It yearns for connection, aches with longing, and expresses itself through tears, anger, and despair. It's the part of us that makes us scream into a pillow. (I've done it many times so my neighbors wouldn't hear my hysterics).

So, how do we come to terms with this tug-of-war between our mind and our heart?

Acknowledge both: don't dismiss either logic or emotions. Give space to both, allowing your mind to seek answers while your heart expresses its pain.

Practice mindful expression: write in your journal, meditate, or use creative outlets to process your emotions without judging yourself.

What I've come to learn is that guilt isn't always rational, but if we can take a step back and at least try to examine it objectively, we can act on it and then let it go. I've learned that sometimes it just requires taking a slow, deep breath in and letting it go, because holding onto long-standing guilty feelings will only keep us in our thought prison and hinder our ability to love ourselves again and find happiness.

As mothers, we feel responsible for our children, even after they've become adults. The mother/child bond will never be severed no matter how old they are. That's why it's important to regularly check in with your emotions and be aware of any lingering guilt.

I remember my grandmother being deeply troubled when her oldest son, my uncle, faced a heart condition necessitating surgery. He was a mortician in a small town and adamant about not undergoing the procedure because he said that he had to bury too many surgeon's mistakes. No amount of logical persuasion from Grandma could sway him. She confided in me back then that, regardless of our children's age, they will always remain our babies. Her words have never rung truer.

I've read several articles from psychologists who say there's a difference between irrational guilt and healthy guilt. They say that irrational guilt refers to a feeling of responsibility or remorse for something that you had no control over or wasn't your fault. They also say that healthy guilt motivates us to learn and grow from mistakes, while irrational guilt is excessive, persistent, and unproductive.

If you're feeling what you think might be irrational guilt after losing your child, it needs to be released. You may find it helpful to read up on it and even see a therapist if you find it's consuming you. You'll learn that it's acceptable to forgive yourself and move forward, because you can't find peace by feeling guilty. We all deserve happiness and healing.

HOW GRIEF AFFECTS YOUR PRESENT MOMENT

"It's OK if the only thing you did today was breathe" ~ *Yumi Sakugawa*

Dearest You,

In the world we're living in today, being in the present moment seems to be challenging for everyone, but especially for those who are grieving. For the vast majority who have lost a child, grief can have a profound impact on our ability to live in the here and now ... to just BE. Here are some of the ways that grief can affect your present moment experience:

Ruminating on the past. During the first few months after Steve died, I found myself constantly thinking about the past, how things used to be, and wishing I could have that life again. This nostalgia made it difficult to focus on the present moment and enjoy the things that were happening around me.

Yes, the memories of your child are important to you, but living back 'there' doesn't allow for being 'here right now.' My uncle, the philosopher in the family, once told me that as much as we will always remember the past, we can't live there. Now I know exactly what he meant.

Worrying about the future. Grief can also lead to anxiety about the future. We worry about how we'll be able to cope without our child, or how we'll make it through the holidays, birthdays, the anniversary of their death, or other "rock your world" events. This, too, takes our focus away from the present moment and makes it impossible to be here now. If you're worrying about those upcoming events, try making a plan ahead of time for those days where you know you're going to be triggered. Since my son's earthly birthday is in March, I start making plans in February for what I'll do on that day to celebrate him. This year, I'm planning on baking his favorite ... a pineapple upside down cake. Will I shed tears as I'm doing it? Yes, but I'll allow myself to cry.

Feeling numb or detached. Grief can sometimes manifest as a sense of numbness or disconnection from the present, making it seem like we're merely going through the motions of life. I compare this to being a character in a zombie movie, detached from our surroundings and unable to engage with the world around us. As a result, we may struggle to develop meaningful connections with others or appreciate the joy that surrounds us if we were to only take a moment to acknowledge it.

Feeling overwhelmed. To say that grief is such an overwhelming experience is truly an understatement. We may feel like we're drowning in our emotions, and it can be difficult to cope with the intensity. It makes it hard to focus on the present moment and appreciate the small things in life. If you find yourself struggling to be present in the moment, there are a few things you can do to help ground yourself:

Allow yourself to feel your emotions. It's important to acknowledge and accept your emotions, even when they're painful. Trying to suppress them will only make them stronger in the long run. Cry if you need to; it helps to cleanse your energy. Because Steve was in my home when his heart attack happened, there are triggers everywhere, so I still keep a box of tissues in every room.

Focus on the present moment. Try to focus on the here and now and on the things you're grateful for. Start a practice of handwriting five things that feel good. It can be as simple as "I'm grateful for this hot cup of coffee" or "I'm grateful for the smile from that store clerk today." This can help you ground yourself and feel more connected to what's going on right now.

When you find yourself stuck. Bring yourself back from the past or projecting into the future by placing both hands over your heart, close your eyes, and take a deep breath in. Release slowly. Do this as many times as it takes to find your 'centered' awareness of the present moment. You may even want to repeat, "I am now here."

Seek support from others. Talking to a therapist or grief counselor with the skill and sensitivity to help you heal, or joining a grief support group can help you process your grief and learn how to cope with it in a healthy way. I've learned some important skills for processing my grief, thanks to being part of a local grief support group.

Take care of yourself. Prioritize restful sleep, eat nutritious meals, maintain proper hydration, and engage in regular physical activity. By nurturing both your physical and mental well-being, you will enhance your overall sense of wellness and presence in the now.

One of the things that helps me stay in the present is the use of essential oils. Sounds odd, maybe, but here are a few of them and the corresponding benefits they provide:

Lemon: Known for its invigorating and uplifting aroma, lemon oil can help boost energy levels, reduce stress, and improve concentration.

Bergamot: This oil has a sweet, citrusy scent that can promote feelings of joy and optimism. Also said to be calming and reduce anxiety.

Grapefruit: Uplifting and energizing, grapefruit oil can combat fatigue and improve mood. It may also help reduce cravings and promote weight management.

Peppermint: This invigorating oil has a refreshing scent that can improve alertness, focus, and energy levels. It may also help relieve headaches and nausea.

Lavender: While primarily known for its calming effects, lavender oil can also promote relaxation and improve sleep quality, indirectly contributing to a better mood.

Frankincense: My personal favorite because I find that it helps to reduce stress and anxiety, and improves my mood.

Here's some additional tips for using essential oils safely and effectively:

- Use only high-quality, therapeutic-grade essential oils. Some are a little pricey, but there's a huge variety at Amazon.

- Dilute essential oils in a carrier oil, such as jojoba oil, coconut oil, or sweet almond oil before applying them to your skin. Or use a diffuser for whole room benefits. If you don't have a diffuser, you can take a few whiffs from the open bottle or put a few drops on a cotton ball and let it sit somewhere close to you. Just don't get the undiluted oil on your skin.

- Do not ingest essential oils.

- Avoid using essential oils on infants and young children.

- If you experience any irritation or discomfort when using essential oils, stop using them immediately.

I've included a link to more instructions and benefits on the **RESOURCES** page at the end of this book.

A GIFT FOR YOUR GRIEVING HEART

"Forgiveness is the greatest gift you can give yourself" ~ *Maya Angelou*

Dearest You,

In the aftermath of losing a child, we often find ourselves in a profoundly challenging state of sorrow. This can make it difficult for those around us, including friends, coworkers, and even relatives, to offer support. Human nature tends to shy away from confronting pain and mortality, which may cause some people to distance themselves.

If this happens, it's essential not to harbor resentment towards those who struggle to connect with you during this time. Their absence may stem from a fear of experiencing similar loss, especially if they have children. Recognizing their apprehensions can help you understand and accept their reactions, allowing for a more compassionate response to their actions.

This situation came up for me with a couple of my friends and a certain family member, all mothers. I'll admit that, at first, I felt abandoned, which compounded the abandonment I felt when Steve died. But I knew deep down that I had to let them off the hook and the only way I could do that was to reverse the roles and put myself in their shoes. That made me realize that they just couldn't make sense of what had taken place in my world.

Because they had never gone through this nightmare, they didn't know how to connect with me and comprehend my feelings. I could tell that they sincerely felt bad and wanted to do something. They just didn't know what to do. At that point, neither did I. But honestly, I completely understood. Once I acknowledged it, I knew I had to let it go.

Why? Because being judgmental is a waste of time and energy and can significantly harm relationships of any kind. It only creates an environment of criticism and intolerance. This leads to feelings of resentment, misunderstanding, and a breakdown in communication, ultimately causing the bond between you and your loved ones and friends to weaken.

Though your journey may feel solitary at times, you're not truly alone. Countless others who have walked this path can provide comfort and direction.

GOD'S BOX OF LITTLE WINS

*"Treat every small victory like you just won the Superbowl" ~ Lewis
Howes*

Dearest You,

I live in the Pacific Northwest where it rains a *lot* in the winter. And lately, it feels like Mother Nature has been shaking her fist at us with one storm after another. Sometimes we'll get little breaks in between, but then she shows up again yelling, "Wait! I'm not done with you yet!" So annoying.

Much like the storm of grief, it can feel like beauty and joy have vanished completely. Some days I find myself begging for just a few rays of sunshine. On those days, it's difficult to find much to be grateful for. But I keep reminding myself that storms don't last forever and, even on a few of the darkest days, tiny sunbeams briefly make their way through the clouds. Finding gratitude, even for the smallest things, can be a lifeline.

Several months into my grief journey, I came across a beautiful box with gold leaf letters that say, "Trust in the Lord." I thought it was lovely at the time I bought it, but set it aside, not really knowing what I'd do with it. I had a lot of other things on my mind at the time.

Then I started taking notice of things I'd been overlooking, like the feeling of warmth from my first sip of coffee. The comfort of my favorite lap blanket that my daughter made from some of Steve's best-loved Hawaiian shirts. The cooing of the doves that gather on the light pole in the morning. The magic of how the hummingbirds flutter their wings while eating at the feeder. The sweetness of a perfectly ripe cluster of red grapes. The fragrance of my favorite shampoo.

That's when I noticed that these simple pleasures were things to be grateful for. Despite my wounds and those pervasive fears about what might be in store for me next, life was still giving me fragments of peace and tranquility to anchor me in the present moment.

So I decided to use my paper cutter and cut strips of pink, yellow, and blue paper to write down the things that brought me a sliver of joy and beauty each day. Just before turning in for the night, I write down the date and say, "I'm grateful for ..." I counted each one as a small win and put them in that beautiful box, shifting my perspective.

This act of noticing things to be grateful for doesn't deny your grief, but rather acknowledges its presence alongside the joys that are still around you. Over time, as I've experienced, it's like planting seeds of hope watered by blessings, even the tiny ones.

Remember, finding light in the darkness is a courageous act and every bit of gratitude is a step toward healing. My "Trust in the Lord" box is now "God's Box of Little Wins."

And when I'm feeling a little wonky, I shake the box, reach my hand in and pull one out to read and I feel better. This seemingly small act shines a light on remembering to be grateful for even the most mundane things. The last one I pulled was that I am grateful for my neighbor who fixed my leaky gutter. Yay!

Experiencing both triumphs and setbacks is a natural part of life. It's important to celebrate your achievements and recognize that every defeat presents a chance for growth and learning. The lessons that come with each challenge contribute to your personal development and resilience. By noticing them, you'll cultivate a mindset that values the little wins, allowing you to grow stronger and wiser with each passing day.

Interesting, isn't it, what our minds can tell our hearts to do and vice versa?

HOOT OWL AND DRAGONFLIES

"Let the dragonfly be your guide, showing you the way to adapt and thrive in the face of change." ~ Chief Seattle

Dearest You,

When my son was in junior high, we lived across the street from a neighborhood park full of tall poplar trees. One day, Steve and his sister were over there and, all of a sudden, came running in the house. "Mom, I need a big towel," he said. When I asked why, he explained that they had found a white owl on the ground, barely breathing.

We grabbed a towel, a cardboard box, and went to see what we could do. We brought the owl home and I called Fish and Game to see if they'd come and pick it up. They said they didn't do that kind of thing, (really?) so I sat with the kids as we whispered a prayer for our dying friend. We all cried as we dug a hole under the tree in the park to bury that beautiful creature.

I tell you this story because for the past three nights, when I get into bed and everything is silent, I've been hearing a hoot owl in the big pine tree next door. It's such a soothing sound and, for some reason, brings me peace.

So I did a little research and found that, in some traditions, owls are considered to be guardians or protectors, and their hooting could be interpreted as a sign that you're being watched over and guided on your path. Other interpretations are that they're considered to be messengers from the spirit world, offering reassurance and support during a challenging time. Because of that experience with the owl in the park, I'm taking it as a signal from my son that all is well with him and the hooting owl next door was sending me a sign to let me know.

But there's more – the dragonflies. Steve knew how much I love them. My fascination with dragonflies came from a time when the kids and I and our dog were exploring the river close to our home. We watched the dragonflies as they hunted for mosquitos, flies, and other insects. It was amazing to see how they could hover, then dart backward, forward, and sideways to catch their next meal.

After Steve died, on the nights I couldn't sleep, I'd be up writing him letters and listening to soft music on my favorite TV music channel. One night, as I was recalling a memory and writing to him about it, a beautiful song I hadn't heard before came on and as I looked up to see the name of it, there was a gorgeous dragonfly with iridescent wings that covered the entire screen. It took my breath away because I knew it was a sign from him. It felt like he was saying, "Hey, Mom, I'm fine!"

From that point on, I began to see dragonflies all over the place, as if they were purposely being put on my path – jewelry, wind chimes, coffee mugs, stickers, ornaments, greeting cards – all kinds of things.

The most striking incident was the day I took some of his cremains to spread in the ocean and, while I was walking to the shore from my car, there was a huge dragonfly painted on the concrete at the end of the parking area. It measured approximately four feet by five feet. Right in front of me! I gasped because I had been to that particular beach many times and it wasn't there before. It was a magical moment and brought me such comfort.

I wish that kind of peace in whatever form it takes for you as well.

UNKNOWN AUTHOR

"Never deprive someone of hope; it might be all they have" ~

H. Jackson Brown, Jr.

Dearest You,

One of my grieving Mom friends found this poem and sent it to me, written by an anonymous author. She said when she read it and saw the reference to dragonflies, she knew I had to have it. I hope you get a glimmer of hope from it as I did:

In a field of shattered stars, where tears like diamonds gleam,

A fragile bud of hope dares sprout, a whispered, sunlit dream.

The air hangs heavy, thick with grief, a shroud upon the soul,

But whispers of your laughter dance, making sorrow lose control.

I see your smile in dragonflies, a fleeting, joyous spark,

And hear your echo in the wind, carried on a rainbow's arc.

The ground beneath my feet feels strange, where once you used to play, but in the rustle of the leaves, your memory lights the way.

Though empty arms ache for your touch, and silent halls resound,

Love's ember glows within my heart, on hallowed, sacred ground.

For hope, like dawn, will kiss the night, and paint the heavens new,

And in the tapestry of stars, I'll find my strength in you.

SUNRISE AFTER RAIN

So I will tend this fragile bud, with tears and whispered prayer,

And watch it bloom to radiant life, a promise in the air.

And though the path may twist and turn, through valleys dark and deep,

The ember of your memory, my child, I will forever keep.

So let the sunlight kiss my face, and wash away the pain,

For hope, like wings, will lift me up, and guide me home again.

SURVIVING THE HOLIDAYS

"I'll always feel you close to me and though you're far from sight, I'll search for you among the stars that shine on Christmas Night" ~ *Unknown*

Dearest You,

There are no "best" tips for surviving the holidays after losing a child. Grief is deeply personal and what works for one person might not work for another. However, I'd like to offer some suggestions that may help you cope if you're dreading the holidays:

Acknowledge your grief and allow yourself to feel: It's okay to feel sad, angry, lonely, or any other emotion that arises. Don't try to suppress your feelings, as this can prolong your grief. Talk about your child, speak his or her name, share memories with loved ones, and cry if you need to. There's no shame in that. Give yourself permission to grieve in your own way and on your own timeline. There's no right or wrong way.

Set realistic expectations: The holidays will never feel the same without your child, so don't put pressure on yourself to participate in traditions or celebrations if your heart tells you it might be overwhelming. It's okay to adjust your plans or even skip them altogether. I've bowed out of more than one invitation to holiday gatherings, explaining that I simply didn't feel up to it. Know that you are loved just for being you and you don't have to do anything to earn it. Communicate your needs and boundaries to family and friends. Let them know if you need space or if there are certain activities you prefer not to do.

Prioritize self-care: Take care of your physical and emotional well-being. Make time for activities that bring you comfort and relaxation. I turned to adult coloring books after my husband died and again after Steve. It helped a lot. I actually found it to be a kind of peaceful meditation. Don't be afraid to seek professional help if you need it. Grief counselors can provide support and other guidance for the holidays as you prepare for them.

Connect with loved ones: Surround yourself with people who understand what you're going through and offer support without judgment. Talk to other bereaved parents, or spend time with friends and family who knew and loved your child. Consider creating new holiday traditions that honor your child's memory. This could involve asking family members to share their favorite stories about them, lighting a candle in their honor, or donating to a charity in their name.

Remember, you are not alone: Many people have experienced the loss of a child, and there are resources available to help you cope. Don't hesitate to seek help from grief support organizations, online communities, or your local faith ministry. I've listed some additional resources that may be helpful at the end of this book, including a grief hotline, available 24/7.

There's no one-size-fits-all approach to surviving the holidays. You will get through this one day at a time. I wish you strength and comfort during this difficult period. Again, I know I've repeated myself often about self-care and finding help in a support group, but honestly, these two things have been the most crucial part of my healing journey, especially during the holidays.

GRACE AND GRATITUDE

"Gratitude makes sense of our past, brings peace for today, and creates a vision for tomorrow" ~ Melody Beattie

Dearest You,

Your heart is hurting but it's pure and full of love for your child. And you may now find that your love feels even more intensified.

Conversely, you may also feel ghosted, abandoned, like what happens when someone just stops talking to you and you can't figure out why. But remember, we're human and it's normal to go through this phase of grief.

At some point, though, gratitude will show up. It's a way of acknowledging the pain of your loss while also finding moments of appreciation for the joy that your child brought into your life. It's a way of honoring their memory while also moving forward step by step. Here are some actions that I've found helpful for grieving with gratitude:

Write a letter to your child. In the letter, express your gratitude for all the ways they touched your life. What did having them in your life teach you? Share your favorite memories of them and how they made you feel.

Create a memory box. Fill the box with things that remind you of them. Things that make you smile, such as photos, mementos, or even their favorite snacks. When you're feeling sad, you can open the box and remember all the good times you had together.

Do something in their honor. This could be anything from planting a tree in their name to volunteering for a cause they cared about. Doing something in their honor is a way of keeping their memory alive and making a difference in the world.

Do an activity, if applicable, that your child loved to do. This could be anything from watching a movie they liked, going for a walk in their favorite park, or cooking their most loved meal. It's a way to connect with their memory, and to feel grateful for the time you had together.

If possible, spend time with people who knew them. Talking to people who knew your child can help you process your grief. It can also be helpful to hear stories about them from other peoples' perspectives. I admit it took me some time to be able to drive by where Steve worked because I wasn't ready to see the parking space where he always parked. Then one day I decided it was time to go in and say hello to everyone and I'm glad I did. It was comforting to hear them say how much they liked him and how he is so missed.

Be grateful that you can express your emotions. Feel the freedom to be sad, angry, or confused. Don't try to bottle up your feelings or wear a fake smile when you feel like crying. I did that in the beginning while I was in shock and ended up getting painful intestinal issues. (I'll spare you the details).

Empathize with yourself and comfort yourself. Say nice things to yourself, about yourself. Indulge yourself with something nice. Buy yourself some flowers. It's okay to smile, laugh, or feel good, even if you are grieving.

Being grateful isn't about erasing the sorrow, but acknowledging the precious gift of having loved and been loved by your child. It can remind you of the strength you possess and the grace of God that continues to surround you. It's not a replacement for grief, but rather a gentle thread woven through your tapestry, offering glimpses of hope and resilience as you travel your new path forward. Remember, gratitude isn't about forgetting the pain, but about finding the courage to carry it with love.

However, if practicing gratitude feels overwhelming right now, be kind to yourself and focus on simply acknowledging your emotions.

WHAT I LEARNED FROM A GOLDEN RETRIEVER

"Being present means being completely aware of all that is. It means you're not in denial, you're not pretending, and you're not avoiding" ~

Debbie Ford

Dearest You,

When I was recently invited to go with a dear friend to bury his Golden Retriever named Loki, who was hit by a car, my first thought was, "How are we going to get through this?"

But I said yes for two reasons. One, I wanted to be there to support my friend during this difficult time. And two, because I had the pleasure of taking care of this furry bundle of unconditional love occasionally, I wanted to say my personal goodbye and thank him for his love and affection.

Another friend, who has a Golden named Lucky, also joined us to say farewell. She, too, is a bundle of pure love. Loki and Lucky spent a lot of time together playing and enjoying life with their humans, who loved and cared for them deeply.

As the guys carried Loki's body to his final resting place, I stayed close to Lucky, held her leash, and just observed her. It was truly incredible to see how she reacted. She sniffed the air as they walked by, probably catching a final whiff of Loki's scent. As they gently laid Loki in the ground, Lucky raised her head for a couple of seconds to the sky, almost as if she was bidding her buddy a fond farewell. And then, without anyone telling her, she simply sat down.

I was in awe, but what struck me the most about watching Lucky is how animals live in the present moment. They don't dwell on the past or project themselves into the future like we humans tend to do. This got me thinking ... could the key to healing from grief be found in our ability to embrace the present moment like animals do?

Thanks to Loki and Lucky, I've gained more insight about my son's passing. The way I see it, I've got a choice: stay stuck and stagnant in the past or continue to heal by reminding myself that life takes place in the present.

Farewell, Loki. I'll never forget our walks together and how, every time you were with me, you made me smile. And thanks to you, I have sticky notes on all my mirrors that say, "Be here now."

Side note – I grew up with dogs and my children did, too. It's painful when we have to euthanize a beloved pet to end their suffering; it feels like we've lost the unconditional love they gave us. However, after observing Lucky's interactions with Loki, it reminded me that all living beings will eventually pass away. Yet, the pure essence of those we love never truly leaves us; it remains in our hearts and consciousness eternally.

WHEN EXPRESSING GRIEF IS DIFFICULT

"Write hard and clear about what hurts" ~ Ernest Hemingway

Dearest You,

As a Mom, you know it's an understatement to say that grief is a complex and overwhelming experience. It's a natural response to your loss, and it can take many forms. When you're grieving, you may feel intense sadness, anger, guilt, abandonment, loneliness, and even physical symptoms.

Unfortunately, the emotions resulting from a significant loss like this can become lodged within your body, making it challenging to process the event. This may result in a significant sense of detachment or numbness, often referred to as the 'grief fog,' which can disrupt your emotional connection and potentially manifest as physical ailments. It's crucial to prevent this from happening to maintain your well-being.

Honestly, expressing my grief has always been a challenge for me with most people. There are times when it feels impossible to share my sorrow with others, causing me to spiral into overthinking. But I have a powerful outlet that allows me to express myself without fear of judgment or being misunderstood – journaling.

It's been a lifeline for me in my process of healing from losing Steve. It has become my safe haven, a space where I can freely delve into my emotions, trace my progress, and find comfort in cherished memories. (In retrospect, there's no doubt in my mind that writing in my journal has also contributed to my physical well-being).

Through the act of handwriting, putting pen to paper, I've been able to navigate the depths of my thoughts and feelings, processing the complex emotions of sorrow and gradually coming to terms with the immense loss I have experienced. By putting pen to paper, I'm able to give grief a voice ... my voice.

The power of journaling lies not only in its ability to provide an outlet for grief but also in its universal applicability, offering comfort and healing to anyone who embarks on an introspective journey of any kind. I was surprised to learn, not long after we were married, that my husband kept a journal of his recovery from alcohol addiction. He said it helped him stay balanced. So you see, it doesn't matter what one is going through, journal writing can be a path to healing and recovery.

Even before Steve's death, writing has been a powerful means of self-discovery and acceptance, enabling me to delve deeper into life's complexities and reconcile with my inner self. This practice has not only fostered a deeper understanding of life, but also equipped me with the means to confront and overcome limiting beliefs and thoughts, what I refer to as my 'shadow side.' (We all have one). The shadow side holds hidden and sometimes uncomfortable aspects of myself that I don't always care to acknowledge. However, this gift of self-reflection through writing has allowed me to embrace my whole self and grow as an individual.

In Julia Cameron's book, *The Artist's Way,* she recommends doing a writing practice called the Morning Pages. What are they? They're three pages of longhand stream of consciousness writing done first thing in the morning. I call them my brain dump, because it's on these pages that I can let my emotions run free with no censor, no inner critic, no punctuation, no perfect grammar, no high school English teacher wagging her finger at me. Often my first sentence is "God, I ask today that you help me with ...."

It's an experience that I believe holds universal appeal, offering the opportunity to delve into emotions and uncover hidden truths. Writing truly has the power to transform, heal, and find peace within ourselves.

A journal or Morning Pages is a safe haven where you can pour out your emotions without reservation. You don't have to worry about others misinterpreting your words or dismissing your pain. In this sacred space, you're free to be completely honest, vulnerable, and raw. And speaking of raw, I admit that there's more than a few curse words on my pages. Shhhh, that's our secret, okay?

The beauty of keeping a journal is that anyone can benefit from this practice, like my husband, regardless of their circumstances or experiences. Whether dealing with the loss of a child, another loved one, the end of a relationship, or any other form of heartache, journaling offers a safe and private space to explore your grief and the lessons you've learned along the way.

One day I was chatting with a friend about my journals and she asked, "What do you imagine your daughter will think when she reads your journals after you're gone?" My answer was two-fold: "When I'm gone, I won't care" and "I imagine she'll learn things about how I processed pain that I could never say out loud."

So, if you find yourself struggling to share your grief with others, I encourage you to embrace the power of journaling. Give yourself the gift of that safe place to express yourself without judgment or fear. Allow the written word to be your companion on the path towards personal healing and understanding. Keep in mind, there are no rules when it comes to grief journaling. The most important thing is to be honest with yourself and simply write what feels authentic to you.

Maybe later ... weeks, months or years from now, you can look back on your journal entries and see how far you've come. And if you do, I sincerely hope you'll give yourself a big hug and say to yourself, "Well done!"

HEALTHY BOUNDARIES

"Setting boundaries is a way of caring for myself. It doesn't make me mean or selfish. It allows me to clearly define what is okay and what is not okay for me." - Unknown

Dearest You,

Placing healthy boundaries is a touchy subject and can be a scary experience, especially while you're grieving. You're already experiencing a feeling of abandonment, so setting boundaries can amplify your fear of rejection, especially if you lean toward people-pleasing. Many of us do this because of our motherly nature. And sometimes the lines can become blurred between empathy and people-pleasing. The reason I bring this up is because I'll be the first to admit that I'm an empath as well as a "recovering" people-pleaser. And setting boundaries was always a challenge until my son died.

Let me explain. At first glance, being an empath and being a people-pleaser may seem similar, but they're actually quite different. An empath is someone who has the ability to deeply understand and feel the emotions of others, while a people-pleaser is someone who seeks the approval and validation of others, often at the expense of their own needs and desires.

Empaths may struggle with setting boundaries because they are so in tune with the needs and feelings of others, but this doesn't necessarily mean they have to be people-pleasers. On the other hand, people-pleasers may have difficulty maintaining their own sense of self and identity, as they are constantly trying to please people to gain their approval. While empathy and people-pleasing both involve an understanding of others' feelings, they are fundamentally different in terms of motivation and impact on our personal well-being.

More often than not, people-pleasing makes it impossible for you to grieve in a healthy way. You're more focused on taking care of others, which means you put your own emotional needs last; and grieving is a wild ride of emotions – no matter what.

Taking a good, hard look at myself regarding this, I did some research and found some eye-opening information from several resources, which all boils down to certain traits which I can identify with and have learned to change:

- **Eagerness to help:** People-pleasers are often very helpful and empathetic, going out of their way to assist others.

- **Fear of disappointing others:** They are highly sensitive to others' opinions and feelings, and they may avoid saying "no" in hopes of not disappointing others.

- **Desire for approval:** People-pleasers are likely to seek validation and approval from others, and may feel rejected or hurt if their efforts are not appreciated.

- **Difficulty expressing their own needs and opinions:** Due to their focus on pleasing others, they may struggle to communicate their own desires and beliefs. However, this behavior can have some serious consequences:

- **Burnout and exhaustion:** People-pleasers often take on more than they can handle, which can lead to physical and emotional exhaustion.

• **Resentment and frustration:** When people-pleasers consistently put others' needs before their own, they may start to feel resentful and frustrated.

• **Low self-esteem:** Constantly seeking validation from others can lead to a weak sense of self-worth and self-esteem.

• **Difficulty maintaining boundaries:** People-pleasers may struggle to set and maintain healthy boundaries, which can lead to being taken advantage of or feeling overwhelmed.

The bottom line is, in its most basic form, people-pleasing revolves around seeking fulfillment through others, which may aggravate the challenges of the grieving process. It's crucial to understand that establishing boundaries is not about isolating yourself or being ego-centered. Rather, it's about safeguarding your own needs and emotional health. Here's how I learned to do it without fear:

Start by identifying your needs and wants. What are the things that are important to you? What do you need in order to feel happy, supported, and healthy? Once you know what you need, you can start to set boundaries that protect those needs when and if you have to.

Understand why you're afraid. What are you afraid of happening if you set boundaries? Hurting someone's feelings? Being rejected or abandoned? Once you understand your fears, you can start to challenge them. Remember the axiom about fear: F.E.A.R. = False Evidence Appearing Real.

You have the right to set boundaries. You are not responsible for other people's feelings or reactions. You have the right to protect your own well-being, even if it means saying no to someone or setting limits on their behavior. Most of the time, we're not surrounded by bad people. It's just that their behavior may make us think twice about what our boundaries need to be.

Be clear and direct with respect. In establishing boundaries, maintain clarity and directness, avoiding being vague or sugarcoating. We can't expect people to read our minds, so express your needs explicitly. For instance, if you require alone time, communicate it assertively: "I understand your needs, but mine are important, too. I need some personal space and time for myself right now." This approach demonstrates consideration for others while stating your own needs.

Be prepared for the possibility of pushback. I've found that most of the time, people are understanding, but it's possible that the other person(s) won't like it when you set a boundary. They may try to argue with you or guilt you into changing your mind. This is a red flag that they don't respect you, so be prepared for this because you may need to stand your ground.

Don't be afraid to walk away. If the other person is not respecting your boundaries, you may need to walk away from the conversation and revisit it later. This is *not* a sign of weakness. It's simply a way of protecting yourself.

Some additional tips that may help you set boundaries without fear:

PRACTICE SAYING NO. Think about the situations or individuals you should begin saying NO to. Regular practice of saying it will make it easier over time. Start with smaller requests and gradually progress to larger ones. If you're not used to saying NO, you might even need to rehearse in front of a mirror, saying it firmly. Remember, NO is a complete sentence, so you don't need to justify it further. Simply saying that one word can be sufficient.

Build your self-esteem. The higher your self-worth, the less apprehensive you are about setting boundaries. Keep in mind that people don't value what they can get for free. They appreciate things that have a perceived value. Therefore, if you're giving your energy without reciprocation, it won't be valued. Balance, with equal give and take, (or close to it), is crucial.

Seek support. If you're struggling to set boundaries, talk to a therapist or counselor. They can help you identify your needs, set boundaries in a healthy way, and cope with any negative reactions from others. Other available options are books, blogs, videos, and additional resources that are free online. Your intuition, which I'll expand on in a later chapter, will also be your guide.

I know setting boundaries might feel counterintuitive right now, but believe me, it's a gift you give yourself when a situation warrants it. I picture it as holding a fragile flame of hope while in the storm of grief. Healthy boundaries will shield that flame, allowing it to grow stronger and illuminate your path forward. This kind of self-care isn't just for your grief journey; it's for having strength throughout your entire life.

HAD I KNOWN

"PTSD is a disease of the nervous system, a consequence of excessive stress. It is not a weakness of character or a lack of courage." ~ Bessel A. van der Kolk

Dearest You,

During one of the grief support meetings I attended, the subject of Post-Traumatic Stress Disorder (PTSD), was discussed and how it can affect anyone who is grieving. Until that night, I had never even considered that it might be affecting me because I always equated it with someone who had served in the military, like my son. He was diagnosed with it a few years after he was discharged from the Army. Had I known then what I know now, I would have given him information on how to help alleviate it, rather than taking the drugs the VA gave him. He stopped taking them because he said they made him feel disconnected with life, like his brain wasn't functioning at full capacity.

Unfortunately, I didn't know until after he had passed that PTSD is affected by the Vagus nerve and how that nerve can affect everything in our bodies, including the nervous system.

But after the meeting that night, I wanted to find out more, so I did some research on it. What I discovered made me recall an incident that happened many years ago when I was going through an enormously stressful time, which made me physically ill. My symptoms included sharp abdominal pain, nausea, increased heart rate, and fatigue. When it happened, it scared the you-know-what out of me, so I went to my doctor as soon as possible. After running some tests, he asked me why I was so stressed and we discussed it. Then he revealed that my

Vagus nerve was compromised, so he prescribed a muscle relaxer. He didn't mention PTSD, but the research I conducted made me realize how little I knew about the impact of stress on the human body. It's surprising that I didn't connect the dots after Steve passed, having had similar symptoms before.

What I learned is this: the Vagus nerve is the longest of the twelve cranial nerves, running from the brainstem down through the neck and chest, and then to the abdomen. It's a crucial component of the parasympathetic nervous system, which is responsible for the body's "rest and digest" response. This alone helped me connect the dots (finally) about what happened back then and what happened after Steve passed, when I wasn't taking good care of myself.

Several articles I read from medical professionals also said that stimulating the Vagus nerve has been shown to have many potential health benefits, including reducing inflammation, which can be beneficial for conditions like rheumatoid arthritis and Crohn's disease. Vagus nerve stimulation can also slow down your heart rate, which can be helpful for people with high blood pressure or anxiety. And don't we know about the anxiety after losing a child???

Some research also suggests that stimulating the Vagus nerve can help to reduce chronic pain, which can be a debilitating condition for many people.

But here's where I *really* had the aha! moment: Vagus nerve stimulation has been shown to have a positive impact on mood and anxiety disorders, such as depression and PTSD. So, looking further, I had to find out just how to stimulate this nerve and discovered five simple things that aren't hard to do:

1. **Deep breathing** - When we're stressed, we have a tendency to take short, shallow breaths. But taking slow, deep breaths

in through the nose and out through the mouth can help stimulate the Vagus nerve and activate the parasympathetic nervous system.

2. **Gargling** - Gargling with water or other liquids can stimulate the muscles in the back of the throat, which connect to the Vagus nerve. I use water with a dash of Himalayan Pink Sea Salt for the mineral content.

3. **Singing** - The vibrations produced by singing or humming can stimulate the Vagus nerve, especially in the throat and vocal cords. Play your favorite songs and sing along!

4. **Cold exposure** - If, like me, you're not a fan of taking a cold shower, you can splash cold water or use a cold, wet washcloth on your face and neck front and back.

5. **Massage** - Gentle, circular massage around the carotid artery in the neck can stimulate the Vagus nerve and may help lower blood pressure and heart rate.

Always consult with a healthcare professional before using any alternative methods to ensure they are safe and appropriate for your specific needs and health conditions.

YOUR SECRET WEAPON

"I believe in intuition and inspiration. At times I feel certain I am right while not knowing the reason." ~ Albert Einstein

Dearest You,

Navigating through life in today's crazy world while grieving can be extremely tough, but luckily you have a secret weapon to help you through the murky waters – your 'Mom' intuition, a.k.a. your inner voice. The key lies in differentiating between the voice of your ego and the voice of your soul, and ultimately, having faith in your soul's guidance. I see it as finding sanctuary in my spiritual source. For me, it's God, where I believe our intuition comes from.

Think of the times in your past when you were clinging to the 'shoulds.' "Maybe I should be further along in my grief journey by now" or "I should be paying more attention to my daily obligations instead of being overwhelmed by sadness" or "I should be praying and meditating more."

The list of 'shoulds' is long and when they come up, are you second-guessing your soul-talk, making a decision to override it? If so, what's the outcome? Did it turn out to be the opposite of your desired result? What if you could make following your intuition a habit, and apply it to your everyday life? I've found that the easiest way to make that happen is to follow a few steps:

Pause and take a deep breath: This will help you calm your mind and create space for your intuition to be heard.

Ask yourself a question: Formulate a clear question you want an answer for, and then wait for your inner response. Feel free to say what I do, "Please show me ..."

Listen to your inner voice: Pay attention to the first thought or feeling that comes to your mind. Your intuition often speaks in whispers, while your mind tends to be loud, more persistent.

Notice any bodily sensations: Intuition often gives bodily signals, whereas the mind tends to lean towards abstract thinking. Commonly, when a situation doesn't feel right, you'll get a fluttery feeling in your stomach, which then moves to your chest, causing your heart to race. That's usually a signal that whatever you're asking about isn't right for you at this time.

Evaluate the response: Your intuition will resonate with your core beliefs and values, while your mind will provide rationalizations or doubts.

Trust the process: Practice this method regularly to strengthen your ability to differentiate between intuition and mind. Over time, you'll become more in sync with your inner guidance system and better able to distinguish between the two. So many times in my life when I haven't listened to my intuition, I was following an old recipe for self-sabotage, constantly overthinking important decisions. Overthinking is exhausting!

Remind yourself to think of your intuition as flexing a muscle that needs to be exercised regularly. Once you realize that your inner wisdom is always right, its influence can extend to every aspect of your life. Decision-making then becomes a whole lot easier, often with more pleasant outcomes. It always makes me smile when I hear women talk about their intuition, while men call it a gut feeling. LOL. They're the same thing.

There's a short poem, written by Christopher Logue, that illustrates a powerful lesson about listening to our inner voice, and embracing the potential for growth and transformation:

Come to the edge.

We might fall.

Come to the edge.

It's too high!

COME TO THE EDGE!

And they came,

And he pushed,

And they flew.

.

What has your inner voice been asking of you lately? Listen and act, because it just might hold the key to a more fulfilling and peaceful journey.

During my grief journey, my intuition told me to stay off of social media as much as possible. Why? Because I noticed it was having a significant impact on my grief, as it often exposed me to various triggers and reminders of losing Steve. The constant stream of updates, photos, and posts from friends, family, and even strangers was bringing up feelings of sadness, anger, and regret. Other mothers have told me the same thing, explaining how they felt compelled to present a positive front while suppressing their true emotions. The truth is that most people don't want to hear about our sadness. I get that, which is why I would rather turn to people in a grief support group who know what this feels like. We can't change anyone else's behavior; we can only change our own.

this feels like. We can't change anyone else's behavior; we can only change our own.

SOMETIMES SHE FORGETS

"Crying does not indicate that you are weak. Since birth it has always been a sign that you are alive." ~ Charlotte Bronte

Dearest You,

It took me a while to start sorting through Steve's things. There were quite a few starts and stops. It was just too hard to tackle that task until some time had passed. So much had changed and so many memories were triggered:

Sometimes She Forgets That He's Really Gone Until ...

SHE SEES HIS MEMORIAL flag draped with dog tags, and remembers the joy and relief she felt the day he came home from serving our country.

She discovers a piece of mail that bears his name and remembers he won't be responding to it.

She hears the low rumble of a pickup truck and remembers it's not his.

She finds his old business card in one of the Sharpie-marked boxes of his life and remembers his dedication to that job.

She finds the Mother's Day cards he sent her and remembers there will be no more.

She smells the aroma of coffee brewing and remembers how they used to sit on the porch and talk over a cup 'o joe.

She sees his work boots tucked away in the back of the closet and remembers the last time he wore them.

She finds his baby pictures in an old photo album and remembers holding his tiny hand until he fell peacefully asleep in her arms.

Then it all comes back. The precious moments of his life from then until now.

She remembers everything.

It's different for every Mom, depending on how old your child was when he or she passed, and there's no right or wrong answer if you feel like now is the right time for sorting through their things – or wait. When you feel the time is right, here are some tips:

Take your time. There is no need to rush through this. Take your time and allow yourself to feel the emotions that come up. Remember, sadness is not weakness so allow yourself to cry. Tears contain those feelings that we shouldn't deny.

Ask for help. If you're feeling overwhelmed, ask for help from a friend, family member, or professional organizer.

Be mindful of your triggers. If certain items trigger your grief, be mindful of them and take breaks as needed. For me, the biggest trigger was Steve's box of cards I had sent him over the years. I didn't know he had saved all of them and it took me a couple of days to come back after that.

Celebrate your progress. As you sort, celebrate your progress. This can help you feel a sense of accomplishment, control, and hope for your future.

Take pictures. You can always snap a picture of something you'd like to keep as a memory, especially the good ones. Doing so may help you to let go of certain items. As you go through the process, you'll know what to keep and what to donate, discard, or give to someone. I let go of a set of RC cars that belonged to Steve and was so pleased that they went to someone who planned to share them with the kids at his church. It was a double-edged sword because it made me feel good that some kids would have fun with them, but I cried as they were taken away.

MAMA BEARS

"A hero is an ordinary individual who finds the strength to persevere and endure in spite of overwhelming obstacles." ~ Christopher Reeve

Dearest You,

When my kids were in their early teens, they took a trip with their dad to Alaska. While camping, they encountered a mama bear with her cubs in the woods. Thank God the kids remained quiet and still, and mama didn't see them or a disaster could have ensued.

As I recalled that memory, I got to thinking about how, in some ways, we're like bears. I mean, who wouldn't like to hibernate, wake up and find out this was all a bad dream, right?

I don't know about you, but I can identify with mama bears now because I think they're heroes in their own right, just as we are. Maybe that's because they actually resemble human motherhood; we're like them in so many ways. So I did a little research to satisfy my curiosity about the similarities between us and them and here's what I learned:

Comparable to the great apes, bears are surprisingly social creatures. And just as human mothers wear a variety of hats, so do mama bears. They're nurturers, teachers, protectors, and fierce defenders of their cubs. This complex level of care and connection holds a fascinating mirror to our own human instincts.

Like us, bears are very social. (If they could talk, I imagine they'd be just as chatty as we are at times). They forge friendships, share resources, and build a sense of community which resembles the bonds that we humans form. Studies reveal a deep well of care within them, especially between mother bears and their cubs. Siblings, too, show a remarkable sense of responsibility, watching out for each other while mama hunts for food.

But their communication transcends words. Much like a human mother's expressive gaze or the gentle touch that speaks volumes, bears use body language, too. A raised paw, a lowered head, a flick of the ears; each gesture carries a message, a story waiting to be told.

And then there's their vision. Bears, like us human mothers, possess an uncanny ability to see everything, even with their backs turned. It's almost as if they have eyes in the back of their heads, just like the old saying goes about us Moms. While their vision may not be a literal 360 degrees, their keen senses and heightened awareness make them guardians, just like we are, always vigilant for any threat to their precious cubs. In essence, mama bears offer a glimpse into the primal depths of motherhood, a shared language of love and unwavering protection that transcends species and speaks to the universal bond between mother and child. Sure sounds like us, doesn't it?

If you're like me, had I known my son was going to leave me behind, I would have been that mama bear who stood up on her hind legs and roared, "Take me instead!"

This poem, by Donna Ashworth – modern day poet, is a beautiful reminder of who we are:

When God created woman he was working late on the 6th day.

An angel came by and asked, "Why spend so much time on her?"

The Lord answered, "Have you seen all the specifications I have to meet to shape her?

She must function in all kinds of situations.

She must be able to embrace several kids at the same time.

Have a hug that can heal anything from a bruised knee to a broken heart.

She must do all this with only two hands.

She cures herself when sick and can work 18 hours a day."

The angel was impressed, "Just two hands...impossible!

And this is the standard model?"

The angel came closer and touched the woman.

"But you have made her so soft, Lord."

"She is soft", said the Lord,

"But I have made her strong. You can't imagine what she can endure and overcome."

"Can she think?" The angel asked.

The Lord answered, "Not only can she think, she can reason and negotiate."

The angel touched her cheeks.

"Lord, it seems this creation is leaking! You have put too many burdens on her."

"She is not leaking...it is a tear" the Lord corrected the angel.

"What's it for?" Asked the angel.

The Lord said, "Tears are her way of expressing her grief, her doubts, her love, her loneliness, her suffering, and her pride."

This made a big impression on the angel,

"Lord, you are a genius. You thought of everything. A woman is indeed marvelous!"

Lord said, "Indeed she is.

She has strength that amazes a man.

She can handle trouble and carry heavy burdens.

She holds happiness, love, and opinions.

She smiles when she feels like screaming.

She sings when she feels like crying.

Cries when happy and laughs when afraid.

She fights for what she believes in.

Her love is unconditional.

Her heart is broken when a next-of-kin or a friend dies but she finds strength to get on with life."

The angel asked: "So she is a perfect being?"

The Lord replied, "No. She has just one drawback...she often forgets what she is worth."

CHILD SUICIDE

"Your memory feels like home to me. So whenever my mind wanders, it always finds its way back to you" ~ Ranata Suzuki

Dearest You,

In my experience of navigating grief, I have personally come across three mothers who have suffered the devastating loss of their child to suicide. It's a topic that's hard to talk about, but it's essential to raise awareness and encourage open dialogue.

I know that, as a mother, there is no greater pain than the loss of a child. But when a child takes their own life, the agony is compounded by the realization that their suffering was so intense, they could no longer bear to live.

The emotions of guilt, confusion, and sadness that follow a child's suicide make mothers question whether they could have done something to prevent it, asking, "Were there signs that I somehow overlooked?" This question can haunt them for the rest of their lives, creating a deep pit of emptiness that nothing can fill.

The grief that follows the initial shock is unlike any other. It's a pain that consumes the very essence of a mother's being, leaving her feeling hollow and broken. There's a profound sense of guilt that accompanies this grief, as mothers often feel responsible for their child's actions. They may wonder if they could have done more to help their child, or if they somehow failed them in their time of need, especially when the child showed no indications of unhappiness or despair.

Even in today's society, where we think we have evolved as humans, there's still a pervasive stigma surrounding mental health and suicide, which makes it difficult for mothers to seek support and understanding following their child's death in fear of being judged by their peers. They feel so isolated and alone, struggling to express their pain and grief. And it may be hard for friends and family to accept the reality of a child's suicide, but it's essential for them to offer their support during this time, acknowledging the unique challenges that come with losing a child in this manner.

In coping with their child's decision, mothers must somehow learn to balance acceptance and respect for their memory. This process demands time, patience, and understanding. Additionally, post-traumatic stress disorder (PTSD) poses an additional significant challenge.

The intense emotions and aftermath associated with their loss can trigger flashbacks, anxiety, and depression, making it difficult for them to move forward. That's the reason it's critical for mothers to seek professional help if they feel consumed by their grief, as therapy, individual counseling, and support groups can provide a safe space to process their emotions and find comfort in the company of others who have gone through the same experience.

The pain and heartache will never fully go away, but with time, support, and understanding, it's possible to find a way to honor their child's memory and begin the healing process. By sharing their stories and getting support, mothers can help break the stigma surrounding mental health and suicide, helping to pave the way for a brighter future for those who are struggling.

To the mothers who have endured this gut-wrenching ordeal, I extend my heartfelt prayers for healing, tranquility, and the knowledge that you are not alone on your journey. You are cherished and supported.

PROFOUND TRANSFORMATION

"I am resilient and I can get through anything." ~ Unknown

Dearest You,

Grief isn't the only battle that people face; there are plenty of others. Some small and some huge. For us Moms, though, losing a child is at the top of the huge pile. In my opinion, everything else pales in comparison.

At some point on your grief path you will, most likely, face what is called the dark night of the soul, as I did in the second year after Steve passed. In my case, I realized I was constantly doing things to keep myself busy so I wouldn't have to face what I now know as my shadow work.

But what is it, really? I'll be honest – it's a challenging and isolating experience to say the least, but it can also be a time of profound transformation and growth. Some refer to it as an initiation into a realm that nothing prepares you for. The truth is that it can sneak up on you before you even realize it's happening.

Does it hurt? Oh, yes! It's like a gaping, infected wound, that hole in your heart that's oozing ghastly, smelly pus. If it isn't cleaned out and a fresh bandage applied, it will only fester and get worse. And yet, it's normal to want to run from it.

However, the dark night of the soul requires *not* suppressing your feelings. You heal by facing, feeling, and releasing your pain. It can be dark; very dark. It may even catapult you into depression. That's when you'll cry. A lot. (I did). But closing your eyes to the darkness (I tried) doesn't get you *out* of darkness. Many times I said, "No, I just can't do this."

But I knew deep down that emotions of fear, anger, bitterness, blame, regret, shame, and grief were hiding in the shadows; lodged in those places I didn't want to examine. Sometimes I felt like a sword had pierced my heart and I was barely clinging to life.

Through prayer, meditation, and journaling, I learned that the only way back to the light was to summon the courage in my soul, rise up in the dark, and walk through it. But there's good news: I wasn't doing it alone. And neither will you. You have a spiritual love team, led by our Creator, surrounding you, who have been with you your whole life. Some refer to them as guardian angels and I've leaned pretty darn hard on mine during all of this.

There's just one catch, though. Creator doesn't mess with your free will and your team isn't allowed to either, so you have to ask for their support and guidance to show you the way, but actually doing the shadow work is up to you. If you're willing, there's a plan and you'll be led. Keep in mind, you're not doing this for other people. It's *your* soul that's opening up.

Of course, because we're here on this earth in human form, naturally we want to know predictive outcomes and how long something like this will last. I wish I could give you a time frame, but that's impossible. It's different for everyone, so it could be weeks, months, or even years.

But it's important to remember that this is not a permanent state. It's a phase that can lead to a deeper understanding of yourself and your place in this world; a world that's different now because of your loss. For me, it was the initiation of healing my mind, spirit, and body.

Coming out of the dark night of the soul, it's possible you could feel more liberated, a little less afraid, more energetic, and more yourself, into a new and brighter phase of your life. Always remember, dear one, the sun never forgets to rise.

FINDING YOUR TRIBE

"Grief changes shape, but it never ends." ~ John Bowlby

Dearest You,

On your grief journey, you'll find that most people are uncomfortable thinking about the death of a child, let alone talking about it. This becomes crystal clear after the initial *I'm so sorry for your loss* time period.

After that, some of your family members, friends and acquaintances drift away. They stop asking questions like, "How are you holding up?" or "Is there anything I can do for you?" They may even change the subject when you want to talk about it. Some will keep their distance completely. But we must forgive them. Why? Because, as I've said in a previous chapter, they don't understand this kind of grief unless they have experienced it.

I certainly didn't understand it 14 years ago when my brother and only sibling died and my mother was going through the loss of her son, like I am now. All I could do was try to help her in ways that I knew how at the time, many of which I'll admit stumbling through. But I listened without interrupting when she wanted to talk about him. We often cried together, yet found ourselves laughing at some of the quirky habits he had, and that helped both of us temporarily in many ways.

Unfortunately, she didn't want to seek help through a grief support group. So I went to one every week, offered by the hospice that took care of him in his last days. My intent was to learn some coping mechanisms and pass them along to my Mom. What I didn't know before the group began was how it would assist my own personal healing.

The facilitator was nothing short of amazing. She made it a safe place for us to open up about our losses, even providing a box of tissues, a big bowl of chocolate kisses, and a bottle of water for everyone at each discussion. The tissues for our tears, the chocolate for our comfort, and the water for hydration.

In the first couple of sessions, most of us sat around the table and just cried. Being vulnerable with each other felt safe because we were all going through it together. I was the only one who had lost a sibling; others had lost a spouse or a child. One had lost both his wife and daughter within a year of each other.

When our guided sessions concluded, the six of us decided that we didn't want our bond to be broken, so we continued to meet on our own once a month at a local coffee shop. We lovingly branded ourselves as the *Gang of Six* and have been friends ever since.

That's the reason it's critical for those of us who are grieving the loss of our child to talk about him or her with people who get it. A grief support system can be your lifeline. I suggest you find a local one with face-to-face meetings. Check to see if their sessions are 'drop-in' so that you can join in whenever you want. If there's not one in your area, you can find support groups online.

As a mother, I have to talk about my son. So do the other mothers and fathers I've met along this new path, which is why a grief support 'tribe' is so beneficial. They've experienced what you're going through, while others who don't understand it might say that talking about our kids just keeps us in sadness. Personal experience has shown me that's not the case. So why *do* we talk about them?

● We talk about them because we're still proud of them.

● We talk about them because they deserve to be remembered.

● We talk about them because, even though they aren't physically here any more, they are never far from our thoughts.

● We talk about them because they will always be a part of us.

● We talk about them because we still love them and nothing will ever change that.

If you haven't found your new 'tribe' yet, search for one that resonates with where this different kind of journey is leading you. Some are faith-based and some aren't. If you find one that doesn't fit you, your intuition will let you know, but keep searching because the right one is out there.

JASPER'S STORY

"Climbing a mountain is not about conquering the peak, but about conquering ourselves, our fears, and our limits. The journey up is as important as the view from the top." ~ Unknown

Dearest You,

Once upon a time in a small village nestled at the foot of an ominous mountain, there lived a brave and determined young man named Jasper. Jasper was known throughout the village for his love of climbing and his never-ending quest to conquer the tallest peaks.

One day, Jasper received news that a group of climbers had gone missing on the mountain that loomed over their village. Despite the danger, Jasper knew he had to act. With his heart pounding and his spirit soaring, he set out to find the lost climbers.

Jasper faced many challenges on his journey – treacherous terrain, raging storms, and countless obstacles that tested his strength and determination. But with each step, he grew more determined to save his fellow climbers.

Finally, after days of searching, Jasper found the lost climbers, huddled together for warmth in a small cave. They were cold, hungry, and exhausted, but Jasper's arrival brought them new hope. With his help, they were able to make their way back to the village, where they were welcomed as heroes.

From that day on, Jasper's name became legendary. He was revered as a hero for his unwavering courage and selflessness. And though the mountain still stood tall and unyielding, Jasper's spirit lived on, inspiring generations of climbers to follow in his footsteps and reach for the stars.

I tell this story because this is like the grief storm on the mountain that you're climbing. Your feet slip, but you keep walking, climbing until you're exhausted; you face obstacles, and there's no clear view of what's at the summit. You're just not sure of your footing anymore and may sometimes wonder if, like Jasper, there's ever going to be a reward for your climb. But, consider yourself a "Jasper" because this is a climb you never thought you'd have to take, yet you haven't given up.

God has been able to use my grief to inspire me to do things I otherwise would have never done, similar to climbing a mountain. He's been able to show me a purpose, a hope, and a joy that I never dreamed would happen, but now can't live without at this point in my life. I'm letting go of the things I thought were important (before my son died) and letting Him direct me to those things that *are* important in order to reach the summit.

My daily prayer: *"God, I ask that you strengthen me, support me, and keep my feet from slipping as I step out and continue climbing this mountain."*

WHAT AM I SUPPOSED TO LEARN?

———

"The weight of regret is heavy on my heart. I wish I could turn back time and rewrite our story." ~ Unknown

Dearest You,

It feels like a gut punch, doesn't it? Even if you knew it was coming, that moment when your child is gone changes you forever. Yet we all know that everything in this earthly realm changes constantly.

These physical bodies that we inhabit must eventually give out. The hard part for us is that we never expected our children's bodies to go before us. However, the soul and consciousness of our beloved children are now free, and they *never* abandon us.

Even when you're able to accept it, your heart may still reach up to your brain and send you messages like, "I wish I had said ___, I wish I had done ___, I wish I could have ___, I should have ___," and on and on.

I call this the *beat yourself up* phase of grief. We all go through it. It's part of the healing path, but nothing is ever gained by beating ourselves up and, as another survivor Mom reminded me, it doesn't change what happened.

When we realize that this death didn't happen TO us, it happened FOR us, that's when we begin to heal. This idea was *really* hard for me to grasp. For the first year, because I was still in shock, I felt like his death happened *to* me and, by no means, did I recognize that there was something valuable I was supposed to learn from it.

When you get to the point, though, where you understand this and can accept it (I know it's tough), you've entered the self-awareness phase of grief. Now you get to ask the question, "What am I supposed to learn from all this?" In a spiritual sense, we are all on a journey of growth and development. But, life often presents us with challenges that can be more difficult than others, much like when a teacher gives a pop quiz on a subject we weren't fully attentive to in class. This can indeed be frustrating, but it's a part of our growth process.

While some find external guidance helpful, others may find deeper wellsprings of healing from within. The key is finding what works for you.

Sometimes your only choice is to surrender your feelings, emotions, circumstances you can't change, and the outcome to a Higher Power. Just offer this, "I surrender my hurt and pain to you. Please guide me to the next right action for my highest good and that of all concerned."

And to your child whom you were blessed to know and love as part of your earthly journey – "Thank you for teaching me so much."

A CURIOUS DIALOGUE WITH GOD

"If it excites you, if it makes you feel good, it's God speaking to you." ~
Wayne Dyer

Dearest You,

Meditation has been a significant part of my life for years, and as I previously mentioned, there were nights when I really struggled to sleep, so I wrote letters to Steve. I began these letters by meditating to quiet my mind, which I refer to as my "monkey mind" (a term we can all relate to).

One evening, the nagging question of *why* Steve passed away before me had me deeply bothered, so I decided to close my eyes, take a few deep breaths, and seek an answer in a state of quiet reflection. Admittedly, my somber mood was more like a demand than just a simple inquiry. This led to an imagined dialogue with God, which may or may not have been influenced by my beliefs about life after death. When I finished writing down the insights that came to me, I felt a sense of peace and calm.

ME: *God, are you there?*

GOD: *Yes, Regina, I'm here.*

ME: *I want to know something. Why did you take Steve so soon?*

GOD: *I didn't take him away from you. He came willingly when he was ready. People seem to think that every human should live to a ripe, old age. That's not true.*

ME: *What do you mean? I don't understand.*

GOD: *Wise people have said that earth is a schoolroom. And it is. Steve learned all he needed there to take the next step for his soul's progression and then he came home to me.*

ME: *What lessons did he learn while he was here?*

GOD: *There were many, but the most important one was to love. You and your mother were his prime examples. As a child, he emulated both of you.*

ME: *I'm confused.*

GOD: *Let me explain. You did the job I gave you when he was born; to show him unconditional love and be an example for him to follow. His soul chose you to be his mother, his first friend, before he incarnated into this lifetime. It was something he needed to learn and had lots of souls to choose from, but his heart knew you would be his best teacher.*

ME: *His teacher? Really? But I felt like I failed him in so many ways. No matter what I said or did, he wouldn't stop drinking.*

GOD: *Please understand, Regina, that all humans develop survival mechanisms when they come to earth. You couldn't have stopped it. Alcohol abuse was his way of coping with dysfunctional relationships. The beings in each relationship wanted more with each other at the soul level, but didn't find a way to express it while in their physical bodies. You see, addictions can morph into behaving like friends and that was the one he chose. Humans will always seek ways to cope with life in the earthly realm. As you've learned, some are more destructive to the physical vessel than others.*

ME: *I understand that now, but there's something more I have to know. Will I see him when I cross over?*

GOD: *I know that's your heart's desire, so you certainly will. And what a celebratory reunion it will be, full of unbounded joy. I'll be there waiting for you, and will throw the party myself!*

ME: *OK, that makes me feel better. I'm not in any hurry to get there, though. You know I don't want to leave yet. Just two more questions. Was he in pain when he died? Was he afraid?*

GOD: *No. Rest assured that his designated angelic guardians who have been with him his entire life were surrounding him as his soul took flight in the split second before his heart stopped beating. It happened so fast that he was a bit confused when he got here, but adjusted quickly when he saw his loved ones, especially his earthly father, waiting for him on this side.*

ME: *Thank you, God. I'm so glad we had this conversation.*

GOD: *I am, too. Thank you for talking to me and for taking such good care of your precious child. And, Regina, please forgive yourself. You did nothing wrong. And don't ever forget that I'm always here for you. Just call on me.*

You may have your own, but my meditation method is really simple if you'd like to give it a try. Just find a place where you'll be undisturbed, get comfortable, light a candle if you wish, close your eyes, breathe in slowly through your nose, hold it for a count of four, and exhale slowly through your mouth for a count of seven. Relax your shoulders as you breathe. You can say or think of any words you like, such as "peace" or "breathe" or "love." Anything that makes you feel good.

Most likely, your monkey mind will try to distract you with all kinds of thoughts and that's normal. Did you know that Stanford University discovered that we have approximately 65,000 thoughts a day? Knowing that, don't beat yourself up if you can't shut them out right away. Just continue to breathe and relax. With time and practice, you'll find meditation has some amazing, soothing benefits. You can also find some excellent free guided meditations on YouTube if you want to start there and also some wonderful meditation apps for your phone.

YOUR WORDS MATTER

"Words are the source of all things. Words have the power to build and destroy. Choose your words wisely." ~ Buddha

Dearest You,

Ever consider the profound impact of the common phrase "I AM?" These two words, often thoughtlessly tossed about in daily communication, can significantly influence how others view you and how you view yourself.

It's true. Think about how often you hear someone say, "I am poor. I am weak. I am depressed. I am sick. I am sad. I am unlucky. I am afraid." Sadly, they're affirming to themselves and the world who they are. Words possess an extraordinary ability to shape our emotions, thoughts, and even our reality. They have the power to inspire, uplift, and heal, but they can also inflict pain, undermine harmony, and create lasting scars. Years ago, my Mom said it was her wish to exit this life, leaving her mark, but leaving no scars.

By carefully choosing our words and using them to express empathy, kindness, and encouragement, we can foster positive connections and nurture personal growth. Conversely, mindless or hurtful language can lead to misunderstandings, hurt feelings, and damaged relationships. Think of the words you choose after "I AM" as brushstrokes, painting the canvas of your identity. They tell the world who you are, what you believe, and what you stand for.

Knowing that, what if you could reframe the above statements to depict a *temporary* condition, rather than a permanent proclamation?

"I am feeling poor right now. I am feeling weak. I am feeling sad right now."

OK, I think you get the picture, right? Our "I AM" statements aren't just pronouncements to the outside world; they also leave an imprint on our inner selves. They shape our self-image, influencing how we approach challenges, navigate relationships, and even make decisions. When we say "I am capable," we empower ourselves to overcome obstacles. When we say "I am worthy," we open ourselves up to love and acceptance.

The power of your words can transform a hesitant "I can't" into a determined "I will." It can turn a negative self-talk loop into a positive affirmation upward spiral. It can even rewrite limiting beliefs that have held us back for years.

So, how can you harness the power of "I AM" for your own good during your grief journey? Here are a few tips:

Choose your words consciously. Pay attention to the labels you attach to yourself. Are they empowering or limiting? Reflect on your values and aspirations, and let your "I AM" statements align with them. "I am making progress every day, even if it's baby steps" and "Even though I am going through this heartbreak, I am divinely loved."

Focus on the present. While acknowledging your past experience of losing your child, remember to ground your "I AM" statements in the present moment. This helps cultivate a sense of ownership over your life. "I am learning how to live in a world without my child."

Embrace the journey. Not everything has to be set in stone. "I am a work in progress" is a powerful statement that acknowledges your growth and willingness to learn.

Celebrate your unique self. Especially when you're grieving, don't be afraid to own your quirks, flaws, and passions. Let your "I AM" statements reflect the beautiful complexity that makes you, you. "I am celebrating the fact that I can grow through all this."

A dear friend of mine shared what her "I AM" statements are when she finds herself feeling down or confused. She calls them her *high vibe* mantra that makes her feel better. I thought to myself, why not? So I tried them and, even though it took some practice and intentional self-belief, I found they work for me, too. And speaking of high vibes, here's what Albert Einstein said, "Everything is energy and vibration. Match the frequency of the reality you want and you cannot help but get that reality. It can be no other way. This is not philosophy. This is physics."

Now, whenever I find myself in a negative thought loop, I place my hand over my heart and say the mantra, borrowed from my friend:

I AM the Light.

I AM the Love.

I AM the Truth.

I AM.

FLASHCARDS

"The true voyage of discovery is not a journey to a new place; it is learning to see with new eyes." ~ Marcel Proust

Dearest You,

As you read in the last chapter, the words we use have a great impact on our well-being. Bruce Lee said, "Don't speak negatively about yourself, not even as a joke. Your body doesn't know the difference. Words are energy and cast spells. That's why they call it spelling. Change the way you speak about yourself and you can change your life. What you're not changing, you're also choosing."

When I was in elementary school, I had a second grade teacher who loved to use flash cards for teaching us new words. And you know what? They worked. I still remember some of them. Haha! I can't believe I do.

Over the years, I've collected phrases and sayings in a notebook that have special meaning in my life. Many of them I've used as writing prompts for journaling. But then, remembering back to second grade, I thought, "Why not make my own set of flashcards from the phrases I've collected?"

So I hand-wrote them on 3x5 cards and randomly chose one each day for inspiration. They have helped me so much on my grief journey and I find it amazing how they apply now, even more than before. It's almost like the universe is saying, "This is what you need to focus on today."

I hope you'll find inspiration from my flash cards idea to make a set for yourself. Feel free to borrow any or all of my favorite phrases:

● I am worthy

● My strength comes from my peaceful inner core

● My angels are supporting me right now

● I am the one I have been waiting for

● I let go of the outcome

● I am limitless

● I am at peace with my past; it has brought me to where I'm meant to be

● I allow myself be happy

● I am free to choose my healing and my light

● All change nourishes my soul

● I possess gifts of the soul that benefit myself and others

● When I replace "why is this happening?" with "what is this trying to teach me?" everything shifts

● The whole purpose of going through an experience is to learn something from it

● I am good at being me

● If it costs me my peace, it's way too expensive

● There's a reason for everything

● It's time for re-invention

- Good things happen to me all the time

- I am right where I need to be

- When it doesn't make sense, I trust in divine timing

- I honor my feelings

- Every day, in every way, I am getting better and better

- I honor my future by choosing to learn from the past

- I have all the tools necessary

- I allow myself to receive

- The Divine is supporting me

- Take a five-minute mental vacation

- I am healthy and strong

- A new path is opening up for me

- Once I choose hope, anything is possible

- I can try new things

- I am enough

- I have meaning and a reason for being

- I notice what's going right

- I only make moves when my heart's in it

● I have healthy boundaries and protect my energy

Your power lies not just in your words, but in the genuine intention and belief you invest in them.

COMPLEX DYNAMICS

"In sharing their experiences and offering mutual encouragement, they help each other navigate through the darkest moments of their lives." ~ *Unknown*

Dearest You,

When Steve passed away, his father had already been gone for three years, leaving me without the support and shared understanding that could have made his loss a little easier to bear. It's clear to me that losing Steve was even harder without someone who truly understood the depth of my grief. That's why I feel it's crucial to talk about how people with different grief styles can impact one another during such challenging times.

If you're currently married, you may be facing or have already experienced some differences in how you and your spouse grieve your child's loss. While both of you may experience similar feelings of sadness, anger, and disbelief, the ways in which you grieve can vary significantly. There can be difficulties and differences that arise when a mother and father are grieving the loss of their child because of their grieving styles.

One of the primary differences between mothers and fathers going through grief is the *way* they express their emotions. We, as mothers, are more likely to seek emotional support from friends and family, as well as engage in activities that honor our child's memory, such as creating memorials or participating in support groups. Fathers, on the other hand, may be more inclined to focus on practical matters, like handling funeral arrangements or returning to work. This difference in grieving styles can lead to misunderstandings and feelings of isolation, as each parent may feel that their partner is not fully understanding their grief. (Sadly, I've heard of marriages that didn't survive after the loss of their child).

Research shows that cultural expectations and gender roles can also play a significant role in the grieving process. In many societies, women are often expected to be more emotionally expressive, while men are encouraged to be more stoic and reserved. These societal norms can create additional pressure for both mothers and fathers, as they may feel that they need to conform to these expectations in order to appear strong for their surviving children or other family members.

Then there's the impact of hormones and biology, meaning that the biological differences between mothers and fathers can also contribute to the unique ways in which they grieve. Research has also shown that women may be more likely to experience depression and anxiety following the loss of a child, while men may be more prone to substance abuse or risk-taking behaviors.

Additionally, the hormonal changes that occur during pregnancy and childbirth can make it more difficult for mothers to process their grief, as they may be dealing with postpartum depression or other mental health issues.

Stuffing emotions will only lead to more difficulties while processing this grief. That's why effective communication is crucial for both parents. It's essential for mothers and fathers to share their feelings and experiences, as well as listen to each other without judgment or criticism. Seeking professional support, such as counseling or therapy, can also be beneficial for you and your spouse, as you work through your grief and learn to support each other during this difficult time.

By seeking the understanding of the differences in grieving styles, cultural expectations, hormonal and biological factors, and communication needs, parents can better support each other and find ways to honor their child's memory together.

It's through open dialogue, honesty, empathy, and understanding that parents can navigate the challenging path of grief and find comfort, hope, and strength in each other's company.

THE HUMAN COMPUTER

"Love is the whole thing. We are only pieces." ~ *Rumi*

Dearest You,

One of the secondary losses I've experienced since my son passed is counting on him for help whenever I had an issue with my computer. He was always there for me when I needed him.

When I was going through his business files, I found a hard copy of a document called *The Human Computer* signed by someone in his office. Apparently she had a crush on him and was trying to drop a hint. I smiled because he was a lovable guy, yet quiet and often shy.

I've included it here because it's message is profound in so many ways for all of us humans currently living on this planet:

Customer: I really need some help. After much consideration, I've decided to install LOVE. Can you guide me through the process?

Tech Support: Yes, I can help you. Are you ready to proceed?

Customer: Well, I'm not very technical, but I think I'm ready to install it now. What do I do?

Tech Support: The first step is to open your HEART. Have you located your HEART?

Customer: Yes, I have, but there are several other programs running right now. Is it okay to install while they are running?

Tech Support: What programs are running?

Customer: *Let's see... I have PAST-HURT.EXE, LOW-ESTEEM.EXE, GRUDGE.EXE, and RESENTMENT.EXE running now.*

Tech Support: *No problem. LOVE will gradually erase PAST-HURT.EXE from your current operating system. It may remain in your permanent memory, but it will no longer disrupt other programs. LOVE will eventually overwrite LOW-ESTEEM.EXE with a module of its own called HIGH-ESTEEM.EXE. However, you have to completely turn off GRUDGE.EXE and RESENTMENT.EXE. Those programs prevent LOVE from being properly installed. Can you turn those off?*

Customer: *I don't know how to turn them off. Can you tell me how?*

Tech Support: *My pleasure. Go to your Start menu and invoke FORGIVENESS.EXE. Do this as many times as necessary until it's erased the programs you don't want.*

Customer: *Okay, now LOVE has started installing itself automatically. Is that normal?*

Tech Support: *Yes. You should receive a message that says it will stay installed for the life of your HEART. Do you see that message?*

Customer: *Yes, I do. Is it completely installed?*

Tech Support: *Yes, but remember that you have only the base program. You need to begin connecting to other HEARTS in order to get the upgrades.*

Customer: *Oops. I have an error message already. What should I do?*

Tech Support: *What does the message say?*

Customer: *It says, "ERROR 412-PROGRAM NOT RUN ON INTERNAL COMPONENTS." What does that mean?*

Tech Support: *Don't worry, that's a common problem. It means that the LOVE program is set up to run on external HEARTS but has not yet been run on your HEART. It is one of those complicated programming things, but in non-technical terms it means you have to "LOVE" your own machine before it can "LOVE" others.*

Customer: *So what should I do?*

Tech Support: *Can you pull down the directory called "SELF-ACCEPTANCE"?*

Customer: *Yes, I have it.*

Tech Support: *Excellent. You're getting good at this. Now, click on the following files and then copy them to the "MYHEART" directory: FORGIVE-SELF.DOC, REALIZE-WORTH.TXT, and ACKNOWLEDGE-LIMITATIONS.DOC. The system will overwrite any conflicting files and begin patching any faulty programming. Also, you need to delete SELF-CRITICISM.EXE from all directories, and then empty your recycle bin afterwards to make sure it is completely gone and never comes back.*

Customer: *Got it. Hey! My HEART is filling up with new files. SMILE.MP3 is playing on my monitor right now and it shows that PEACE.EXE, and CONTENTMENT.EXE are copying themselves all over my HEART. Is this normal?*

Tech Support: *Sometimes. For others it takes a while, but eventually everything gets downloaded at the proper time. So, LOVE is installed and running. You should be able to handle it from here. Ah, one more thing.*

Customer: *Yes?*

Tech Support: *LOVE is freeware. Be sure to give it and its various modules to everybody you meet. They will in turn share it with other people and they will return some similarly cool modules back to you.*

Customer: *I will! Thanks for your help!*

(Author unknown)

TESSIE

―――

"When angels visit us, we do not hear the rustle of wings, nor feel the feathery touch of the breast of a dove; but we know their presence by the love they create in our hearts." ~ Mary Baker Eddy

Dearest You,

As I mentioned in the beginning, I knew I would never be able to have another conversation with Steve, so to keep from losing my mind, I started writing him letters which were later published.

In order to put this into context, I'd like to share one of the letters I wrote to him after my encounter with a woman named Tessie, who I believe is an earth angel, sent by God with a message just for me. It blew my mind how it happened and was proof for me that miracles *do* happen and they *are* real:

Dear Steve,

Even now as I'm writing this, I have goosebumps. The reason is that today I believe I came face-to-face with one of God's messengers ... an angel in the flesh named Tessie.

It wasn't raining so I had the urge to go to the park beside the hospital where they took you. I just wanted to walk for a while with the sun's warmth on my face and feel the soft moist grass under my feet. I could actually smell the earth's sweet fragrance and it felt good.

On my way back from the park, I decided I'd better stop by the supermarket and pick up a few things. Normally, as you know, I like to shop at Winco because it's employee-owned. Not like those big chain stores.

But then I got another urge. I was guided to go to Walmart, and I don't even like Walmart!

My first thought was NO, but for some reason, I went anyway. I guess I've learned during this grief journey to pay attention to these 'nudges.'

I kind of had an attitude when I walked in, but I bit my lip, grabbed a cart and headed toward the food department. About halfway there, I noticed a lady who was hugging a fuzzy sweatshirt to her face. I stopped, smiled, and said, "That looks really warm and cozy."

She responded with, "Yes, I must look pretty silly holding it like this, but I'm cold all the time and want something warm to sleep in, so I was testing it." We both laughed and continued our conversation. She was so endearing.

At one point, our conversation turned to discussing our children and grandchildren. And how she asks Jesus all the time to watch over them. I confessed that I do the same thing every day.

Keep in mind, you know I don't believe in 'accidents.' Neither did you, Steve. Then she told me about a dream she had where Jesus was standing at the top of a grand staircase, both arms outstretched, welcoming a long line of people who were advancing toward him. The way she described it, I had a clear picture immediately.

She was in line with a toddler, holding his hand. She said what was odd to her is that she didn't even know the little boy. But when they got to the top and stood together facing Jesus, he smiled, placed the palm of his hand on the top of her head, and said, "It's not your turn yet. I'll take care of him now."

Tessie saw the tears in my eyes, held out her hand to me and I took it. It was so warm and loving, and at that moment, I realized her message was for me. I knew in my heart that our meeting had been synchronized by Divine design.

I have often questioned why you died before me, Steve. As you know, I would gladly have taken your place. But never has the answer been clear until I met Tessie ... it's not my turn yet. Only God knows when that will be.

IT'S ABOUT TIME

"Time is not money. Time is your life. Spend it wisely." ~ Harvey Mackay

Dearest You,

One of the most valuable lessons I've learned during my grief journey is how and with whom I spend my time and what's most important to me. And like the above quote says, *time is your life; spend it wisely.*

As mothers who have endured the tragedy of losing our children, we have the extraordinary privilege to fully embrace our individuality and cherish this incredible gift of life. Time, our most valuable asset, is not to be squandered, for its scarcity only serves to highlight its importance. Not knowing when our own journey will end, we must make the most of our days and choose wisely how we spend our time.

Grasp this understanding and allow it to spark a flame within you, urging action and cultivating positive change in your life and the lives of others. Seize the day, as the timeless saying Carpe Diem suggests, and make every moment count towards the realization of your dreams and the betterment of the world around you.

All of the insights below may not apply to your current situation, but if there's even one that helps you see your life now from a different perspective, then that one missing piece might complete the puzzle of your purpose, revealing a vibrant and fulfilling life ahead.

Reflect on this: are you truly spending your time in a way that aligns with your deepest desires? Or are you spending your 'currency' doing these things?

- Chasing approval (the only validation you need is that of your Creator)

- Worrying about things out of your control (worry doesn't change an outcome)

- Judging others (nope, that's God's gig)

- Engaging in negative self-talk (that will rot your brain)

- Comparing yourself to others (comparison is the biggest thief of joy)

- Pleasing everyone (there will always be someone who doesn't like you no matter what you do)

- Dwelling on past mistakes (robs you of your peace)

- Investing in one-way relationships (leaves you feeling drained, unsupported, and unappreciated, eroding your self-esteem)

- Not letting your feelings out (even the ones that scare you)

- Overthinking every decision (your intuition is your greatest asset; follow it)

- Spending time with energy-drainers (establish clear boundaries to limit your interactions with these people)

- Chasing perfection (breeds anxiety and stress and can damage relationships)

- Saying yes to everything (can lead to feelings of exhaustion, irritability, and resentment)

- Drama (don't try to fix someone else's problems)

- Chasing money at the expense of happiness (ignoring what's really important in life)

- Waiting for the right moment (becoming paralyzed by indecision)

- Constantly refreshing social media feeds (keeps you in FOMO = Fear Of Missing Out)

Spending time wisely to discover our purpose in life is invaluable, as it allows us to gain clarity on our goals and aspirations. We're still here for a reason and by understanding our purpose, we can focus our energy on pursuits that bring us fulfillment and ultimately lead to personal growth, harmony, and happiness.

I love this quote from Eckhart Tolle: "You are present when what you are doing is not primarily a means to an end (money, prestige, winning), but fulfilling in itself, when there is joy and aliveness in what you do."

This life of ours is only a short trip – enjoy it.

FINAL THOUGHTS

"Happiness is a choice, and we can choose it no matter what our circumstances." ~ Anita Moorjani, author of Dying to Be Me

Sister, I know the storm you've weathered. The downpour of grief that has etched itself into your soul, the hollow ache that echoes in every beat of your heart. But I also know the resilience that's within you, that strong flame born from love that can never be extinguished.

To support your emotional balance during your journey, I've provided a brief overview of essential factors to consider. This summary is designed to be a handy reference, so you can quickly review it without having to go through the entire book again:

Acknowledge and Accept Your Emotions: The first step in finding emotional balance during grief is to acknowledge and accept your emotions. It's important to recognize that it's okay to feel sad, angry, or even numb. Grief is not linear, and you may experience various emotions at different times. Honor them, and allow yourself to feel them without judgment. This acceptance will help you process your grief and move forward.

Establish a Support System: Grieving can be a lonely experience, but it doesn't have to be. Lean on your support system, which may include family, friends, and/or a support group. Having someone to talk to about your feelings can be incredibly therapeutic. Additionally, consider seeking professional help from a therapist or counselor who specializes in grief counseling if and when you feel the need. They can provide guidance and support during this challenging time.

Practice Self-Care: Taking care of yourself, loving yourself, is vital during the grieving process. Engage in activities that nourish your body and soul, such as eating well, getting enough sleep, and exercising regularly. Additionally, make time for relaxation and stress-reduction techniques, such as meditation, yoga, or deep breathing exercises. Self-care will help you maintain emotional balance and cope with the stress of your loss.

Establish a Routine: Grief can disrupt your daily routine, leaving you feeling lost, disoriented and lonely. Establishing a new routine can provide structure and stability during this challenging time. Set aside specific times for self-care, socializing, and engaging in activities that bring you joy. This routine will help you find and maintain a sense of normalcy and create a solid foundation for emotional balance.

Express Your Emotions: There are various ways to express your emotions, and finding the method that works best for you is essential. You may find writing in a journal or participating in creative activities, such as drawing, painting or music, to be therapeutic. You may also find comfort in talking to a friend or seeking spiritual guidance. Experiment with different methods to find the one that resonates with you and helps you process your grief.

Give Yourself Time: Grief is sometimes described as a process, but a process normally has an end point. I describe it as a journey full of twists and turns, and it takes time to heal. Be patient with yourself and understand that it's normal to experience ups and downs. Don't rush the healing path or compare your grief journey to others. Allow yourself the grace, time, and space to grieve in your own way and at your own pace. This isn't a sprint; it's a marathon.

Conclusion: Managing emotional responses to grief is a personal journey that requires patience, self-compassion, and support. By acknowledging your feelings, seeking support, establishing a routine, practicing self-care, honoring your loved one, giving yourself time, and seeking professional help when needed, you can navigate the storm of grief and find your way to healing and growth. Trust that you *will* find emotional balance once again.

Even though we've never met, it's been my honor to share what I and other mothers have learned on this journey. I hope that during the course of reading this book, you've found helpful insights on how to take good care of yourself, and ways to avoid the pitfalls of grief burnout. Always remember – even after the rain, the sun never fails to rise again, painting the sky with hues of healing and love, a testament to your enduring maternal spirit. You are the only one who knows the correct path to take, so rely on your intuition as your most trusted compass, guiding you through healing, personal growth, and self-awareness.

A new beginning is ready to be explored, lived, and experienced. Go forth, dear sister, and let your own *Sunrise After Rain* illuminate the world. You are so loved and needed.

Much love and many blessings,

Regina

RESOURCES

Listed below are some resources that you may find helpful on your journey:

Online Memorial Website to Honor Your Child:

https://www.forevermissed.com

Grief Support Services/Groups:

https://www.griefshare.org

https://healgrief.org/grief-support-resources

https://griefhaven.org

5 Best Online Grief Counseling Services of 2024:

https://www.forbes.com/health/mind/best-online-grief-counseling

Grief Hotline - 24/7 support: 1-800-221-7437

https://firstcandle.org/bereavement-support

How to Mix Essential Oils and Carrier Oils:

https://oilsforwellbeing.com/how-to-mix-carrier-oil-and-essential-oil

RECOMMENDED READING:

The Power of Now - A Guide to Spiritual Enlightenment, by Eckhart Tolle

The Artist's Way - A Spiritual Path to Higher Creativity, by Julia Cameron:

Poems, Books, and Inspirational Gifts by Donna Ashworth:

https://donnaashworth.com

Anita Moorjani, best-selling author of Dying to Be Me:

https://www.anitamoorjani.com

My Letters to Steve Book:

https://grieflifelines.com/readingnook

About the Author

Regina Arnold, with a heart for helping others, has dedicated over two decades to supporting individuals in the staffing sector.

However, life took an unexpected turn when she faced the heart-wrenching loss of her son. This tragedy led her to refocus her writing career, where she now draws from her personal experience to offer comfort and guidance to those journeying through the complexities of grief.

Through her heartfelt books, such as "Sunrise After Rain," Regina has found solace in her writing. Her creative spirit extends into both fiction and nonfiction, enriching the lives of her readers.

When she doesn't have her hands on the keyboard, Regina enjoys the beauty of the Oregon coast, capturing precious moments through photography, enjoying connections with the canine world, and embracing new adventures with friends.

To learn more about Regina and her journey, including her touching tribute, Bye for Now, P.J. - How Writing Letters to My Departed Son Moved Me from Broken to Better, visit her website.

Read more at https://grieflifelines.com.

www.ingramcontent.com/pod-product-compliance
Lightning Source LLC
Chambersburg PA
CBHW022144150726
47992CB00002B/743